Connecting to Spirit
If you build it, they will come

a skeptic discovers true meaning of the afterlife

Bob Dean / Kathleen Tucci
with contributions from Larry Hastings
a near death survivor

Connecting to Spirit – if you build it, they will come

PRINTING HISTORY
First printing paperback edition / October 2004

This book is an Intuitive Psychic publication and is available at special quantity discounts for bulk purchases for sales promotions, premiums, fund-raising, or educational use. Special books, or book excerpts, can also be created to fit specific needs. For details, write:

Unique Markets Bob Dean / Kathleen Tucci
2828 Parker Road, Suite B106e
Plano, Texas 75075-9159

World Wide Web site address is
http://www.connectingtospirit.com

ISBN 0-9728973-1-3

PRINTED IN THE UNITED STATES OF AMERICA

10 9 8 7 6

Dedicated *to my daughter*

Laurie Ann

who crossed over in 1980, and gave me the incentive to continue in my pursuit.

Contents

Acknowledgment
Introduction
Preface

PART 1 – *They don't know what they don't know*

PART 2 – *Addressing the questions and drawing a road map*

PART 3 – *How newfound awareness shapes lives*

Resources

Acknowledgement

To John Edward

Thank you John, for introducing and connecting us to the spirit dimension. It is more than we could ever have even imagined.

The Cover

The basis of the book cover is actually a photo taken by Marianne Ball Dean, award-winning artist of oil paintings and porcelain art, including one from Walt Disney's Festival of the Masters.

Her original photo appears below, untouched, and clearly showing two angels formed by the clouds.

For the cover, we have added the light, which represents the path to the afterlife as seen and described by those who have had near death experiences...and the orbs, which represent spirit energy. (Cover revisions thanks to Woody Sanders.)

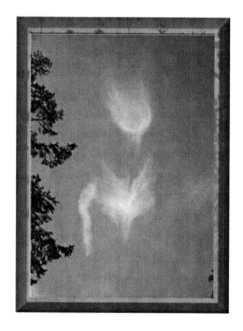

Introduction by Kathleen Tucci

My work as a medium has led me down numerous paths. Although I have always been a "healthy skeptic" I am very "aware" of when I'm being led in a new direction by the powers that be. One path that started as a side road has since turned into a highway of new information brought to light by my good and dear friend Bob Dean.

Our association has continued to convince us both that our lives are mapped out to a certain degree and that our work here on Earth, both collectively and individually, is certain to change many lives.

My thirst for information and answers on how the spirit world works, why we are here, and what we are to accomplish while living in this physical presence has brought me to several conclusions, yet at the same time this thirst has opened the door to more questions.

Witnessing Bob's spiritual journey and studying near death experiences as well as analyses from hundreds of readings has provided insight to questions such as:

How do we blend organized religion with what most refer to as paranormal spirituality?

How do we determine if it was really our loved one's "time" to cross over to the spirit realm at physical death?

How does a medium, or anyone for that matter, have the ability to speak to a spirit if that spirit has been reincarnated?

Why do deceased loved ones, in the "normal" world, not show us any signs that they are okay and around us if there is an afterlife?

What determines one person's ability to be so much greater than the next, when both individuals are educated and versed in spiritual communication?

In terms of levels of consciousness there are many determining factors, both metaphysical and scientific, that explain many of these nuances. So much of what we can and do experience with the spiritual realm while in an earthly existence relates to the law of physics. Yet there are many unexplainable occurrences that indeed validate for us that spiritual existence continues after physical death.

In this book, I provide you with a psychic and spiritual perspective on his experiences and also those encounters and events that I have myself endured. You'll enjoy the richness of how "spirit" has pushed our lives together, a skeptic and a psychic, and how we have since been shifted to work together to share our knowledge of what we've found. We will touch on such subjects as…

- Why we all have a Master Spirit Guide and several lower level guides that assist us every day.
- Why contact with our guides and angels is vital to our progress both here on the earth and in spirit.
- What tasks that deceased loved ones have once they are on the other side.
- Who is the counsel of elders and why they are important to our destiny here on earth.
- Specific tools available to everyone that are "keys" to making multi-dimensional communication possible.
- Why the accuracy of information provides true evidential proof that the phenomena of channeling a loved one exists…and much, much more…

It is my opinion that the linear earthly plane and the universal spiritual plane are not two separate worlds of existence. They are, in fact, resonating together, simultaneously illuminating each other's presence.

Bob's Background

I am presenting a short biography of my life and careers here because it has significant relevance to the journal, and the journal will refer back to many of these time periods and events.

1952 - 1956 Attended Lyman Hall High School, Wallingford Connecticut.

1956 My dad (Charley) crossed over from alcohol poisoning.

1956 - 1957 Attended Boston University School of Aeronautical Engineering.

1957 - 1961 Attended US Air Force Academy, Colorado Springs, Colorado.

1957 Best friend in high school, David Stevens, crossed over after his jet crashed during his last week of Naval Aviator Training.

1961 - 1962 Pilot training at Vance Air Force Base, Enid, Oklahoma.

1962 First daughter, Laurie Ann, was born.

1962 - 1966 Pilot for Air Training Command flying T-29's at James Connaly AFB, Waco, Texas.

1964 Second daughter, Lynda, born in Waco.

1966 - 1967 Served one year in Viet Nam in the 315th Air Commando Squadron.

1966 Awarded several Air Medals, the Bronze Star, and Distinguished Flying Cross.

1966 Third daughter, Sheri, born in Connecticut.

1966 My best friend and roommate, Stan Cox, crossed over when his plane was shot down.

1967 - 1989 Pilot for Braniff Airlines based in Dallas, Texas. Went bankrupt second time in 1989.

1968 Divorced from first wife Karen, children's mother. Remained friends.

August 16, 1980 Oldest daughter **Laurie Ann** crossed over.

1990 - 1996 Corporate pilot flying out of Love Field, Dallas.

1992 Married current wife Patty.

1999 – 2002 Lear Jet pilot for AmeriPlan Corp, Dallas. Retired from full time flying in March 2002.

September 2000 Unintentionally began journey into Spiritualism.

Preface

In September of 2000, when I first watched John Edward on his first few Sci-Fi shows, I assumed he was a fake. But after a few weeks of shows I became more intrigued by his accuracy, and I decided to investigate the "afterlife" phenomenon with an open mind. My research took several directions. Such as:

(1) Reading all of John's books, plus books by other mediums like Sylvia Browne, Suzane Northrop, George Anderson, and Kathleen Tucci. Plus other related books on Yoga, hypnosis, out-of-body experiences, near death experiences, reincarnation, and reading case studies of people who have received after-death communications (such as the book *Hello From Heaven*).

(2) Reading the books and going to the websites of former skeptics like Victor Zammit, and studying up on more "scientific" approaches to the afterlife such as the University of Arizona's study on mediums. (Which I also followed up by email to Professor Gary Schwartz, the head of the study, for his personal opinion.)

(3) By ordering the John Edward meditation tapes and learning to meditate, so that I might participate with a "hands on" approach.

(4) By seeking out and finding someone who actually had a genuine Near-Death Experience (NDE) and talking to him at length about his experiences, beliefs, and changes in attitude. And also to determine first hand if his experience is consistent with the books and accounts of the legitimate mediums.

(5) By seeking out a referred medium myself, and going to her for the experience of seeing for myself if a "reading" is valid, and learning the mechanics of how it is done.

(6) By reading articles of medium critics like Michael Shermer and the "Amazing Randi" to see if they had uncovered anything

substantial or legitimate to counter the phenomenon...other than the obvious goal of making money by trying to debase a rapidly growing field.

The endeavors above were all that I had *planned*. However, to my great surprise and total bewilderment there came actual "contacts" with the spirit world in various ways and incidences that have actually happened to both my wife and myself, and including contacts that have involved friends and relatives that can be absolutely verified.

After 12 months of pursuing these studies, I have come to the conclusion that there IS an afterlife and there IS a "spirit dimension". In fact, there is not one bit of doubt in my mind...it does exist.

My wife, Patty, and I have personally experienced many situations that confirm and re-confirm the conclusion. In addition, the folks in the afterlife are able to contact us through various means that I will describe in this journal in detail.

Here is what we have learned about the spirit world from our continuing "adventures."

Spirits are somehow related to or composed of energy forms, and they are either a creation of God or actually a part of God Himself. Spirits ARE NOT manifestations of humans. Rather it is just the opposite. The spirit is eternal, the indestructible soul, the origin...and the spirit lives at "home". The life here on Earth, the human, is an incarnation of the individual spirit, and Earth is merely a temporary residence. Therefore, the human consciousness does not die. The human body may die, but the spirit merely goes back "home", which is where it started out.

"Home" can be called heaven, a parallel dimension, or whatever you want, but in any case it is a much better place than Earth. Spirits carry on with their lives just as we do here, but there is no disease, hatred, bigotry, religious conflicts, or tragedies such as we suffer on Earth, and the presence of God is felt everywhere.

Materialistic pursuits are non-existent in their world, but the pursuit of spiritual advancement is continuous. (Why Earth was even created is a mystery to me, except that it appears to be a place of "continuing education" for them.)

Everyone on Earth has at least one spirit guide, but most do not know it or do not care. Most humans don't have the time or the determination to pursue this area, even if they are curious. There may be more than one guide, and some guides could be relatives who have crossed over.

NOTE: Spiritual leaders in other countries like Tibet, India, and China (especially Hindu and Buddhist Sects and also I might add, native American Indians) have known this information for hundreds of years but they really don't seem to care if the rest of the world figures it out or not. Certain Yoga sects are also very connected to the spirit world. We westerners have always tended to call these folks "weird", but in truth, we are just ignorant and they are the ones with the knowledge.

Under certain conditions we can communicate with spirits and they can communicate with us. In other words, we can breach each other's dimension through energy forces. Their communications can take many paths, such as electrical or appliance disturbances, telephone contact, subconscious or conscious input to the human brain, the movement of objects, and on occasion an actual appearance in some energy form but usually in the likeness that they had on Earth. Their energy force operates on a higher frequency level than ours can normally achieve. However, at certain times or under certain conditions, the frequencies can come close enough for a valid contact.

For a few gifted humans, usually called "mediums", spirit communication is more easily attained and often at will. For most humans, a contact is a rare occasion and may only occur shortly after a death or during stressful situations. Humans do however have the potential and ability to develop the energy power necessary to meet the spiritual frequencies usually by meditation and right-brain conditioning. This is NOT easily achieved and most humans do not have the patience, time, desire, or confirmed belief to work with it. It is quite possible that spirits try to contact us a lot more often than we realize, but we are just not listening or tuned in. The bustle of everyday life interferes greatly with such potential contact.

Reincarnation is a fact. On a scientific basis, there are thousands of noted cases where people under hypnosis can remember portions of a past life. There is a good chance that a spirit will incarnate back to earth in another human body, but not in any other form. (We cannot come back as animals.) Although it is somewhat disputed, it appears that some people MUST come back to earth for "continuing education", while others have reached a spiritual level that allows them a choice. (Larry's spiritual guide told him that this is probably his last forced incarnation. You'll read more about Larry in coming chapters.)

This level of awareness about the afterlife that I have achieved does NOT interfere with any logical or established religion. In fact, this awareness has strengthened my belief in God, but just in a different way than some religions preach. I can be comfortable in any church of God, except those that border on the radical fringes. This awareness has made me much more at ease with religion in general, in the sense that the different religions are really different paths to God Himself and that no one religion is better or "more right" than any other. In the spirit world, they know this...it is WE FOLKS ON EARTH who have screwed things up and made life more complicated.

Having said all this, here is my story of adventures, how I came to these conclusions, and my entry into the spiritual world. A world that I did not even believe existed until I decided to open the door, and they answered.

Bob Dean

❖ *Part One* ❖
They don't know what they don't know.

Chapter 1 Confirming Skepticism

Follow along as Bob Dean's story unfolds to reveal fascinating and compelling conclusions about the afterlife. In the form of his factual journal as he wrote it, you'll be captivated by the essence of pure scholarship as he travels the path from skeptic to believer.

This manuscript explores what happens to those of us who, while just ordinary people, fall into extraordinary circumstances and beg to ask the question… "What now?"

After his journal, I provide a few chapters on Spirit Guides, dreams, physical death, and thoughts about developing higher spiritual awareness. I will also cover a more detailed account of the NDE of Larry Hastings.

Kathleen Tucci

October, Year 2000...the journey begins

Basically, I have always been a skeptic and a critic. I love to tear movies apart and pick on fakers. My wife Patty gets very flustered during an action movie where there is an airplane involved, because I will yell "They can't do that! That is impossible on an airplane." Patty would say, "Well, normal people don't know that. Stop ruining the movie!"

I really liked to pick on the so-called "psychics" that advertised on TV...like Miss Cleo. I was always amazed at how so many people could fall for that garbage.

It's not that I completely disbelieved in everything. I always left the door open to psychic phenomena, like ESP and spirits and ghosts. I just figured since nothing ever happened to me personally, I'll just keep a curious eye on the subject. My philosophy was there are too many fakes and charlatans out there, and it was a subject area in which I could probably never make validations or take part in on a personal level.

(Hang on...things were about to change.)

It all started one day when I saw a new TV show advertised on the Sci-Fi channel called *"Crossing Over"* with John Edward. He was a psychic medium who could communicate with the dead. (Yeah, right.)

"Hey Patty...let's watch this show on tonight...it's about some guy who talks to dead people."

"Oh Geez," she said, "He's gonna have a ball with this one."

We watched the show, and John certainly was entertaining. I kept my "skeptic mind" working overtime to try and figure out how he was doing these "readings".

(The Bruce Willis movies and the airplane movies were a lot easier to trash. This guy is going to be really tough!)

We continued to watch every show for the next few months, and the more we watched, the more convinced we were that this guy *really could* communicate with spirits. There just was no possible way he could be a fake. He involved too many people, and he was, for the most part, deadly accurate (no pun intended) with his validations. Through these spirit communications, he even knew things about folks that were family secrets, or such things as tattoos on their thigh. Not to mention that he was very entertaining.

Now comes the interesting part. After watching several months of John Edward, we figured...okay...we're open to the concept that a spiritual dimension exists, and we can communicate with them. If so, this is quite a startling revelation. But how can we investigate this further? And for what purpose?

We started by ordering John's first book "*One Last Time*". Fascinating. So we then ordered his second book "*What If God Were the Sun.*" These books just aroused more curiosity, so we ordered five more books on mediums and ADC's that John and other sources had recommended. As we read these books, we came to realize that ADC's (After Death Communication) and NDE's (Near Death Experience) were a lot more common than we thought, and...a lot more interesting.

But one thing really stood out. *All the authors were saying the <u>exact same thing</u> about the spirit dimension, the NDE's, the ADC's, and the manner in which spirits exist and operate.* There was not an iota of difference. How could they all be describing the exact same dimension in the exact same detail? Were they all in a huge "medium conspiracy?"

I scanned the internet often, searching for more information, and I found a lot of sites that were into this afterlife phenomenon. One of the best sites was that of a skeptical lawyer, Victor Zammit, who did extensive historical and scientific research in the area, and finally came to the conclusion that there were legitimate mediums out there who were not deceiving the public. His site became a reference point for my "continuing education".

Journal Discussion: March 2001

Well...reading these books is fine, and it has created a fascinating new "hobby" for us. But now comes the question.... how can we actually become involved in this?

To be a really true believer, I want these spirit folks to contact ME! I need some *personal* happenings or occurrences. Also...where can I find someone to talk to who has actually had a near death experience? More and more questions came to my mind.

Patty and I had many relatives and friends who had crossed over, and we would sure like to make some contact with them. We kept them in our thoughts. My daughter Laurie Ann, who had died in 1980, was my top priority, but we decided not to be fussy. Stan, my pilot friend and roommate in Viet Nam was killed when his plane crashed. David Stevens, my high school best friend had passed also, who's plane had crashed on his last week of Naval Aviator training.

Patty had two close friends, elderly ladies, who had recently died. Patty's sister's husband Bobby, died suddenly last February. Both of our fathers died a long time ago.

(One good thing about this hobby...there's no shortage of subjects. I am also thinking...if John Edward and about 15 other legitimate mediums in this country can communicate with the dead, and they say that we *all* can do this, what a challenge! Hey...I want in!!!!)

John Edward explains that we have to learn to meditate and bring our energy frequencies to a higher level. So I began to do meditation exercises from a few tips in one of the books. Later, I ordered John's meditation tapes, which are full of tricks to help get into a meditative state.

After a while, I began to learn that this meditation stuff is a lot harder and much more comprehensive than I thought. And it's going to take a lot *longer* than I thought. But...what the hell. Meditating a couple times a week should be enough. Patty and I began to "joke" about it at night before going to sleep..."don't forget to meditate while you are dozing off and send these folks a phone call. Tell them to contact us."

(This sounds a little flippant, but we actually were starting to take this stuff seriously. Little did we know that we were really going to get some help here.)

Journal Entry: Monday, March 5, 2001.....midnight

Close encounters of the first kind.

We were in bed fast asleep. The house had been secured...including the burglar alarm. Our bedroom door was closed. We already did our regular routine..."Call the spirits...ha ha...let's see if they are listening."

We had been asleep for some time, when Patty shot up in the bed and said, "Someone is in our house!!!! Do you hear that?"

I rose up and listened. The clock said 12:01. Sure enough, there was a very loud "hissing" sound coming from the main part of the house. **OH GEEZ!!** (I had been burglarized twice in the past.)

I got up and grabbed the loaded .38 I keep in the dresser drawer and headed toward the door. I peeked out.... nothing. I told Patty to stay put. I crouched down, crawling on the floor stark naked, and started to sneak out of the bedroom......pistol cocked. The sound appeared to be coming from the office, which is two rooms away. I crawled toward the office, pistol aimed at the door.

Lo and behold, the office TV had *turned itself on* at midnight...full blast...on a channel that had no program!!

Now...how can this TV turn itself on? It was 5 years old, and never did that before we got into this spirit stuff. We both just shook our heads and went back to bed. I said to Patty, "You know? Those spirits must be laughing their ass off at me sneakin around like that."

Was it an electrical fluke? Or was it the beginning of "contact"? Time will tell. I am still a skeptic.

Journal Discussion: Monday, March 12, 2001

Well...turning on the TV is a nice trick, but what else can they do? Besides, don't those folks know that we have to sleep here on earth? I was wondering if they could please play the tricks during daylight hours. Or...maybe I have to learn to meditate better.

John had some tapes available titled "**Developing Your Own Psychic Powers.**" They contained meditation exercises and information about what he does and how you can do it also. So we ordered them.

Journal Entry: Friday, March 16, 2001

The plot thickens.

Background info: I am a corporate pilot for a Dallas company, flying a Lear 35 Jet. From March 15 to March 18, I was in Philadelphia on a layover. I had a company cell phone for that month. I charged it up overnight and unplugged it in the morning.

Meanwhile, back home in Carrollton, on March 16, Patty went to bed at home and fell asleep around 10 pm.

Patty tells her story:

On the night of March 16, Bob was on a company layover. I had watched TV and turned it off to go to sleep. I had set the house burglar alarm, which I always do regularly when I am home alone.

I had been asleep for a couple of hours when I was awakened but unaware of what woke me up. There hovering about two feet over the foot of the bed were two sets of out stretched arms each holding hot pink roses. The one on the left had dozens of hot pink roses from the wrists of their hands all the way up the arms almost to the shoulders; the one on the right had about half as many roses as the other, but also all the way up the arms from their wrists to their shoulders. The vision was not transparent or ghostly, but the arms looked solid and fleshy, just like two real persons.

I was positive I was awake, and looked at the burglar alarm light to make sure it was on and wondered how someone had gotten into the house. I could see the atrium light from the slits in the blinds in both the bedroom and the vanity area so I know I was awake and was not just dreaming.

I was so shocked that I screamed out, and the arms with the roses disappeared before I ever got a chance to look up and see the faces. My heart felt as if it was beating out of my chest, and after I calmed down a little, I went to the bathroom and got back in the bed and tried to comprehend what I had just seen. It was the most amazing experience I have ever had, and I will always remember how the roses were a very vivid hot pink.

I decided to tell Bob about this event tomorrow when he calls.

Bob's story now...Saturday, March 17

Meanwhile, back in Philadelphia, I got up around 9 am and checked the cell phone. Oops. The LCD display area was completely blank...just a green screen. I tried everything to get it working. Buron, the other pilot, came to my room later and looked at it also, but he just said it was broke, and forget it. I just threw it in the suitcase.

Two days later....Monday, March 19...at home...7:30 am.

Remember, the cell phone quit working the same night as Patty's vision. Patty is preparing to go to work at 8 am, and I was preparing for a day off. Patty's lunch, ready to go, was on the counter right next to the broken cell phone. I wasn't charging it now; I just threw it on the counter till I could take it back to the company.

While Patty was eating breakfast, I picked up the cell phone and said to her: "You know? If those spirits are so good with electricity, why don't they fix this phone?"

Patty: "You know? If you don't stop harassing them, they're gonna come down here and kick your ass." We both laugh.

7:57 am... Patty is walking out the door. I yell, "Wait...here's your lunch." I then happened to glance at the cell phone...all the digits were back!! I picked it up and yelled to Patty, "Hey look at this!!" I called Buron on it to see if it worked, and the call went right through. "Hey Buron, you won't believe this, but the phone fixed itself!!" (Or did it?)

Patty (with a smug *I-told-you-so* look) got into her car and took off for work.

Electrical quirk? Or contact number two?

Journal Entry: Monday, April 9, 2001

Patty's story... Second time.

It is now a couple of months after my sister's husband Bobby, passed away suddenly. He had a distinct, recognizable voice.

I was awakened from a deep sleep by his voice calling my name. I sat straight up in the bed to see where the voice was coming from. I woke Bob up when I sat up in the bed and he asked what was wrong. I told him that I had heard Bobby's voice calling my name "TRISH" (a name that only my immediate family calls me). I never saw anything, but definitely DID hear HIS voice and I know I WAS NOT dreaming.

Journal Entry: May, 2001 (unable to recall exact date)

I had a daughter, Laurie, who died in 1980 while I was on a trip during my Braniff years. I included her in some meditations. During one particular meditation, I asked for a sign from her. Maybe I should be more specific, I thought. I needed to ask for something uncommon, so I would know with more certainty. Then I thought of her beloved horse, Jasmine. During a meditation, I asked that this name would somehow come to me loud and clear over the next few days....a sign that she was okay. Then I would know. It is not a very common name.

I got one of her paintings down from the closet and hung it up. It was her favorite painting...a Braniff 727 flying through the clouds, and she wrote some nice words to me on the back. I was really thinking about her. But there was no Jasmine that day. Maybe this would take a while.

The very NEXT day we were watching John's show, and about in the middle, John was receiving spiritual communications for someone in the audience. His comment went something like this... "They're telling me either Aladdin or Jasmine. Do you have any connection with Aladdin or Jasmine?"

There it was!!! He said Jasmine and Aladdin three or four times and stressed it. And the weird part of it? Jasmine was NOT the word that was involved...it was Aladdin. Jasmine had nothing to do with the communication. Perhaps it was just there for me.

(Coincidence? Maybe. But these coincidences are really piling up now.)

Journal Entry: May 20, 2001

One step from the loony bin.

Not much activity going on in May. But I happened to remember that my now 87-year-old Mother used to tell me an "angel story" about my grandmother, Elsie Toelle. Over all these years when mom brought the story up, I just said, "Yeah, right mom. You're one step from the loony bin." But now I think it appropriate to re-visit mom's story with a little different attitude. So I called her and asked her to write it to me in detail.

Background:

Elsie, my grandmother, was a peach of a lady. I remember her well. When I was a kid, mom and my brother Ronnie and I lived with her and grandpa for a year when mom was divorced and couldn't afford a house. Elsie was very spiritual and kind, and wouldn't hurt a fly. In 1963, Elsie was only 67 years old, and in good health.

Also...some story data here.....grandma had a very old music box that *used* to play a tune. But it had been broken for many years. My grandfather could fix cars, machinery, just about anything, but he could never get that music box to work again. Grandpa also had a lot of property that went well into the woodlands. The property had a creek, woods and hills.

<u>End of May, 2001...mom's letter came in the mail...this is Mom's story:</u>

In April of 1963, I stopped in to visit my mother (Elsie) in the late morning. She said to me, "Evelyn let's take a walk into the woods. I have been going down there and there are angels hovering above. The music they are playing is beautiful and you can even hear their wings fluttering."

I didn't really feel like going down there, so I just said, "Let's just have a cup of tea." I went home after the tea.

(I later learned that she also told a church member about the angels.)

Two days later, Elsie died of a heart attack and passed away. I regret my decision about not going to the woods even to this day.

A couple weeks later, I was visiting grandpa, and he played the music box. He said, "It just came on by itself a few days after Elsie died."

A month later, grandpa died.

(Note: From the book *"Séance"* by Suzane Northrop...Chapter IV *"Both children and the elderly seem to have a foreknowledge of their deaths...again within three days of death. It's during this three-day period when angels are seen..."*)

MORE of Mom's story...years earlier.

(**Note:** I was one of the "kids"...and Charlie was my father.)

I was divorced from Charlie, but I still cared for him, and we saw each other frequently when he came to get the kids. On August 2, 1956 Charlie died of cirrhosis of the liver. We all went to the funeral.

A day or two later I was waking up in the morning and lay there on my back before getting out of bed. All of a sudden I looked up and saw Charlie standing by my bed, looking down at me. He was dressed in a suit, had a big smile on his face, and the swelling and yellow color of the disease was gone. He looked so happy and was a perfect picture of health. *I am sure* I was awake, and he came to tell me he was ok and well now. This incident really comforted me, and made it easier to accept his death. The vision lasted only a few seconds.

I told mom that I was looking at things in our lives a bit differently now, and that I would no longer threaten her with the loony bin.

Journal Entry: Monday, June 18, 2001

They're baacckk.

Background Info: In our bedroom, there is a 35 inch TV on an étagère...across the room from the bed. Below the TV is a clock radio with large red numbers. We never set an alarm, and we always wake up automatically at 6:20 to 6:30 in the morning. We just glance at that clock to confirm the time. We have never used the radio feature.

At 11:35 pm: We were asleep. For some strange reason we weren't sure if it was a noise, or what, but Patty and I raised our heads off the pillows at the same time and looked at the clock. It was blinking 1204. The blinking would normally mean that the electricity went off in the house, and came back on.

We both got up and went into the main areas to see how much damage was done (meaning we had to re-program ALL the clocks, the coffee maker, and check the computers). Well the computers said the electricity did NOT go off, and all the other clocks were working fine.

I jumped back in bed, and Patty went over to re-set the clock radio. It is still dark in the room. Suddenly, some preacher in a very loud, booming voice filled the room with "Praise the Lord, Praise be to God!!" And he kept repeating that, over and over.

I said "Patty, turn that thing off!"

She said, "I hit the wrong button, but I can't find it to shut it off. Turn on the TV so I can see." Meanwhile...the booming voice continues with, "Praise the Lord. Praise be to God!!"

So...using the men's remote control (as in most households, there is no women's remote), I turned on the TV. Well it went on, but the tube was dark, there was loud static, and a green "8" was in the upper right corner. Now we've got loud TV static PLUS, "Praise the Lord!!" And still no light for Patty. I got out of bed and went over to the light switch, and turned on the ceiling light. Now the TV would not shut off. Preacher was still preaching. Static still hissing. And Patty was sitting on the floor laughing. (Brain flash: Maybe we ought to forget this spirit stuff and try a NEW hobby.)

I had to unplug the clock and TV from the wall to shut them off. After plugging them back in, everything worked normal, and Patty set the clock. This had never happened before, and has not happened since.

I could not see any possible way that the electricity could have gone off just to that socket. And it may *not* have gone off, but something surely spooked the clock and TV.

Journal Entry: Friday, June 22, 2001

How'd they do that???

At 9 am...I sat down in the living room recliner chair to read a couple chapters of *Hello From Heaven*. I just happened to look up at the ceiling and right near the fan was a beautiful angel made of reflected light, complete with body, legs, head, and beautiful wings. It was looking down at me. It had a complete circle of light around it and a halo around the head. Absolutely mind-boggling.

It was the sun coming in the picture window and reflecting off of a cocktail table next to the couch. On the table is a little metal car with a plant in it (Patty's new creation the day before) which interfered with the reflection off the table and caused the angel image on the ceiling...but just how it caused such a perfect image I don't know. (Except that the car plant had to be <u>perfectly</u> located in that spot and the leaves had to be shaped exactly right).

It lasted 15 minutes...until the sun went too high.

I took 4 pictures of it. Every day now, between 9:00 am and 9:15, an angel crosses our ceiling.

Journal Discussion:

Okay, now I am thinking...what is the significance of this angel? I don't really know. But if I were to guess, I would say it was a message that we were on the right path and that someone up there really is keeping an eye on us.

(Later...that next month it dawned on me. Three of the books I read said to "schedule" meditation periods at the same time every day, and in the same place, which I had not been doing. Apparently, the angel was a guide that served as a reminder every morning at 9:00 to 9:30 am.)

Journal Discussion: Monday, June 25-30, 2001

I am beginning to learn that this meditation thing is going to take some time for me to get the hang of it. I figured that in the meantime, I would sure like to talk to someone who actually died, experienced the fringe of the afterlife, and then came back (Near Death Experience, or NDE). But I had no idea how to go about finding someone like that. So...I threw the idea into the meditations, but as the days wore on, I gave up on it. I figured they weren't listening to me. Maybe I am meditating wrong. Maybe I have to go back to John's tapes.

Journal Entry: Thursday, July 12 through Sunday, July 15, 2001...they heard.

There are two of us Lear-Jet pilots for our company. We had a trip leaving Thursday for Lebanon, Missouri, where the boss bought some property. We were coming back Sunday at 6 pm.

Now, Lebanon is a friendly little town, but not very much to do. So being the one who gets the hotel rooms, I booked the Sheraton in Springfield, one hour away. There's a lot more to do there.

Our plan was to land in Lebanon Thursday evening and drive to Springfield, then drive back Sunday afternoon at 3 pm to eat and check out the town and hotels at that time, to see if there was more to Lebanon than appeared.

Thursday night, 6 pm

Checking the weather in Dallas, it said Lebanon had clear skies and would remain clear all night. No problem. However when we were 15 minutes from our Lebanon landing (8:15 pm), the Air Traffic Controller told us that Lebanon had *suddenly* been covered by clouds and the visibility was deteriorating rapidly.

We tried an approach, which SHOULD have been a piece of cake, but the visibility was so low that we could not get in...and we tried twice. We then we diverted to Springfield, a few minutes away by air, and where the weather was fine.

(The plot thickens.)

We told the boss (Daniel) and his wife (Dana) that we would get them a room at our hotel and fly them to Lebanon in the morning. Then we pilots would drive back to Springfield.

Meanwhile, after landing in Springfield, Daniel invites us for dinner at Applebee's, across from the Sheraton. Here he talks us into canceling the Springfield hotel and staying in Lebanon Friday and Saturday so he can show us his property.

(Well...sometimes it is wise to say yes, even when you don't want to.)

So...the next day we flew to Lebanon and got rooms at the Hampton Inn.

(What this is doing is setting up some circumstances that would substantially affect the purpose of this story.)

For the next two days, we took in Daniel's new property and toured little ole Lebanon. On Sunday, the Hampton hotel was filling up for that day, so we were forced to check out at 1 pm. Since we already toured the city, the early checkout meant we just go eat and spend 3 hours at the FBO (terminal for corporate pilots) reading, watching TV, or doing crossword puzzles.

Chapter 2 Meeting Larry

Sitting around at the FBO: After reading a couple magazines, I decided to go out to my luggage in the jet and get my book *Hello From Heaven*, which is almost finished now. As I was coming back into the FBO, the gal who runs it on Sundays (Kathy) looked at me and said, "Excuse me.... what is that book about?"

I said, "Well...ahem...uh...ah....it's about near death experiences and after-life communications." (I was a little hesitant, because most people think this stuff is a little hokey.)

She said, "That's what I thought. We have a pilot here in Lebanon, based at this FBO, named Larry Hastings who died for 20 minutes and then shocked the entire hospital by getting up and walking off. He told me about the experiences he had while he was supposed to be dead. Is that what you are reading about?"

I just about fell over, "Yes, can you call him for me?"

And she did...and Larry was home, and we talked for over an hour. Absolutely fascinating... my first real contact with someone who had an NDE.

He related the whole story....floating around above his body and watching them try to revive him...the tunnel...the light...meeting his spirit guide...everything, <u>exactly</u> as it is explained in the books.

We made plans to meet again next week, as we were scheduled for another Lebanon trip from Friday noon till Sunday afternoon.

Journal Discussion: Now this whole story came about by a series of <u>very unusual</u> circumstances, starting with a mysterious "sudden" cloud over Lebanon and ending with a lady who was curious about my book.

Had we stayed in Springfield, I would not have been reading that book at the FBO. And this was the FIRST time since working for the company that we ever had to divert to another airport.

Coincidence? Maybe...but these "coincidences" seem to be piling up a little too regularly. And now I am beginning to see just how the "folks" up there work. Amazing!!

Journal Entry: Monday, July 16

The power of a woman's spirit guide.

Patty wants to go to Lebanon to see Larry and his family also. I asked Daniel, and he said she could go if there is a seat left. The next day, Karen (the scheduler) said the Lear was full...seven folks going. Patty still puts in for Friday off. She said, "My spirit guide will find a way...hide and watch."

Late Thursday afternoon, Karen called me and said one passenger dropped out, and Patty is a GO. (Now...how did I have the feeling that this was going to happen?)

Saturday, July 21...Lebanon, Missouri

Patty, Buron and I went to Larry's house for dinner and discussion. We met his wife Elizabeth and two lovely, very intelligent daughters....Crystal and Laura...12 and 14. (They even laughed at my jokes.) The whole family acted like we were all close friends and we knew each other forever. We felt very close to them immediately.

After dinner, Larry told us his story. He died in the hospital after he was given a second drug that did not agree with the first drug they gave him. They tried the shock boards, and by this time, Larry was floating above them, trying to tell them that he was not dead. However, they finally declared his body dead and put the sheet over him.

Meanwhile, after floating around in a confused state for several minutes, he was finally led through a long tunnel at a tremendously fast speed. At the end of the tunnel was the bright light, where Larry felt extremely safe and in a state of pure ecstasy and love. Here he felt the presence of a spiritual being who told him in telepathic form that he must go back...that his life on earth was not over yet, and he had much more to do. He protested that he did not want to go back, but the being explained that this was not a choice.

Before he left, the being introduced him to the "universal knowledge" which included spiritual love and understanding, and gave him the gift of automatic writing. The being said he would stay in contact with him on earth through automatic writing and lucid dreams.

Larry was then whisked back through the tunnel, and back into his body on the operating table.

Larry said the staff was just stunned beyond words as they watched a person who was dead for 20 minutes just throw off the sheet and sit up.

Then Larry brought out hundreds of pages of his automatic writing, dating back 18 years. The writing was hard to understand at first, because there were no spaces or punctuation and none of the i's were dotted and none of the t's were crossed. But it was readable once I got the hang of it. The gist of the writing was how to live a better life here on earth and much guidance for Larry's future. Larry also learned that his spirit guide was named Joshua.

Larry said that each person has a spirit guide, but most people do not know of it or do not care. He said that once you seek contact with the guides, you become open to their guidance, and that "coincidences" will happen to you often. (Like being in Lebanon instead of Springfield.) Larry added that our loved ones that crossed over can definitely take a part in our earthly lives, that they often watch us, that they *can* communicate with us through various means, and that they often can help us by way of the "coincidences".

I asked about the existence of God, and he said God was on a higher level than spirits and angels, but God's presence was everywhere. And that there is no such thing as religion...that whatever "religion" you are, you are going to the same place when you cross over. So it really doesn't matter.

He also talked of reincarnation, and that under certain circumstances you are able to come back to earth as another human being. Some people MUST come back because they had not completed their purpose or lessons on earth during their previous life or lives. Most do not want to come back, because it is so peaceful and beautiful there. Joshua told Larry that this would probably be his last tour of duty on earth.

When Buron, Patty and I left the Hastings' home, we were totally stunned at what we had encountered. That night.... as I began a meditation to sleep.... I realized that once again that the folks up there came through, just as I had asked, and even better than I could imagine. BOY!! This stuff just gets better and better!!!

Journal Entry: Monday, July 23, 2001...7 pm

Hey guys...you forgot the VCR's.

Normally we tape John Edward from 7:00 to 8:00 pm central time, and then watch him later so we can zip through the commercials. We have 2 VCRs, one in the bedroom and one is a combo-TV in the office. Been taping John for 6 months.

I entered the tape just as always in the bedroom VCR, and it swallowed the tape and shut itself off. The only way to get the tape out was to unplug it, plug it back in, and the VCR came on for 4 seconds, then shut itself off again. I had to eject the tape in those 4 seconds.

I took the tape to the office VCR and entered it. This time, the VCR ejected the tape and shut off the TV. Well...must be a bad tape. I got a new tape out, but the results were the same on both TV's. I got a little flustered then. Even Patty tried it....no dice. So we couldn't tape John.

I kept thinking about this, so at 9:30 pm I decided to try and tape something off of the bedroom TV with the same tape as before. *It worked fine.* I took the tape to the office...that worked normal too. Go figure. This has never happened before our spiritual quest, and it hasn't given us a problem since.

I asked Patty why they didn't want us to tape John Edward. She said, "Because they wanted to booger the VCR's, and that is the only time you use them." Hmmm. She always has an answer. What can I say, she's had a visual visit by two spirits, and I haven't.

Journal Entry: Sunday, July 29, 2001

I called my Aunt Arlene in Florida to tell her about Larry's experience. Arlene was a spiritualist long before I knew what that meant, and she acquired much of her knowledge from Sylvia Browne, a medium like John Edward. I called her about 5 months ago on this subject, but I wasn't as heavily addicted yet, so she was too advanced for me.

We talked about an hour. Her beliefs are *exactly* the same as what I have learned this past year. She even knows who her spirit guide is. She said I should order some of Browne's books...which I did.

Journal Entry: Monday, July 30, 2001

Patty's Story...back seat driver??

("**Some accounts of the spirit world suggest that our deceased loved ones may have foreknowledge of some human events and, if appropriate, can alert us to threatening situations.**" *Hello From Heaven*, Chapter 19.)

I was coming home from work, driving north on Marsh Lane, which is a 3-lane highway. I always drive in the right lane, because the other two lanes have the craziest drivers in them trying to get home from work.

I was driving in the right lane as usual, with a car to my left and a string of cars behind me. It was traffic hour, and I do not like to change lanes.

But for some reason, I suddenly got a *very strong intuitive feeling* to go immediately to the middle lane. I was happy where I was, so I just ignored the feeling. Then it came to me again, and much stronger, so I immediately slipped behind the car in the middle lane that was to my left.

About 25 feet later, that car in front of me in the middle lane suddenly made a right turn to go into a 7-11 parking lot. He flashed across the right lane, and the car that was earlier behind me in the right lane smashed solidly into his passenger side.

If I had stayed in the right lane, it would have been *me* that he whacked. I have learned from reading the books that those "strong feelings" should be heeded.

Chapter 3 Evaluating the Info

Journal Entry: Saturday, August 4, 2001

I had this past week off, and did some meditations in the morning, Wednesday and Thursday. During one of them, I decided to ask for another sign from Laurie. So this time I asked for her name to come to me loud and clear...and in an unusual situation...and spelled L-A-U-R-I-E (most are spelled Lori or Lorie).

Now, I do not go looking for the signs; I just figure they will come unexpectedly.

On Saturday, Buron and I had to drop off the Learjet in Houston for a week of maintenance, and then we had to fly back to Dallas on Southwest Airlines. In Houston, as we were checking in to come back, there were two agents at the desk. Buron went to the girl, who was doing a crossword puzzle. (Light traveling night, obviously.) While Buron was buying the tickets, I started working on her puzzle. After the purchase, she came back to the puzzle and all three of us were working on it for about 20 minutes. She had long hair, which covered her nametag, and she was very nice and friendly.

She went to help another customer, and then came back to the puzzle...but now I could see her name tag...LAURIE!!!! I said, "I have a daughter named Laurie, and it is spelled just like your name."

She replied, "Yes, it is not usually spelled this way, but the real test is....what is her middle name?" I told her it was Laurie Ann. She said "Yep...that is my name...Laurie Ann"

Bingo!! A bonus too.

Journal Entry: Saturday, August 11, 2001

Another layover in Lebanon, Missouri and a 3-hour chat with Larry Hastings. Since the last get-together, I have read even more about the afterlife, so I was prepared to find out if he was in agreement with the books I have been reading. I had some pretty tough questions to ask him this time. Here are a few.

Me: Larry...when you meditate, who are you talking or praying to?

Larry: Whomever you want. God...or you can ask for help or answers from your spirit guide. They will hear you, but they answer you when they feel like it. They have a lot more things to do than chat with you every day, unless you are in a bit of trouble. And they usually know that ahead of time.

Me: You said you didn't know who Sylvia Browne or John Edward was...aren't you interested in learning more about the afterlife?

Larry: No....not from psychics here, although there appear to be a handful of legitimate ones. I got all the information I need from Joshua and other guides through automatic writing and through lucid dreams. Why read books when you can get it first hand.

Me: Many who have had near-death experiences seem to have come back with other psychic powers. Did that happen to you?

Larry: To some degree. Back in my hometown in Wyoming, a plane was lost for two days in the mountains. I was told where that plane was in a dream, so I called the sheriff's office and led them right to it, and it was right where the dream said it was. Stuff like that. I also get "intuitive feelings" about things occasionally, like something about to happen. And twice, one of my "lesser" spirit guides...it wasn't Joshua...brought me on an "out of body" experience, but I don't like doing that, so I told them to quit.

(Note: From the books I have been reading, reincarnation is a given. Sometimes you have a choice, and other times you MUST be reincarnated if your past lives did not fulfill the lessons of God's plan. I am interested to hear more of what Larry says about this.)

Me: Larry...do you believe in reincarnation?

Larry: Oh, yes. We have all had past lives, except angels. Joshua had told me about who I was in one past life, but he also told me that this life now will probably be my last "forced" reincarnation, as long as I continue to fulfill my plan here on earth.

Me: Will you come back again voluntarily?

Larry: No way. You cannot imagine how much better it is at "home". This earthly life is very tough in comparison, and way too materialistic. In the spirit dimension, you feel God's presence all the time...and it is a most beautiful world. No prejudice, no wars, no fighting, no problems. Everyone is equal and there is unconditional love. In pilot's terminology, this place on earth sucks. (We laugh.)

Note: From everything that Larry and I discussed that afternoon, I did not find one iota of difference from what was presented in the six books I have read.

Journal Entry: Tuesday, August 14, 2001

Buron and I had a 3-day layover in Jackson Hole, Wyoming, carrying Texas Senator Tom DeLay and his family. Now...Jackson is beautiful and very quaint, but it is a BIG tourist trap. Nothing much for me to do there but go walking and jogging, eat, read, and meditate. (Although last night we attended Tom DeLay's barbeque party.)

On Tuesday, I had already gone out walking twice, and in the early afternoon I did some meditation for about 20 minutes. It is always relaxing. Among other meditations, I decided to ask for one more sign from Laurie again...but loud and clear and right here in Jackson. (I am *really* putting the pressure on those spirit folks now!)

Then I decided to go for one more walk before dinner...this time around some of the side streets. I was nearly lost for a while there, several blocks off the main drag. But as I reached a corner and waited for a WALK light, I looked up at the corner building which said in great big letters, LAURIE...Interior Design. (Well!!! What took them so long?)

Now I am thinking...no one is going to believe this *again*. But then I thought, I'll bet this store advertises in the phone book. When I got back to the hotel, I dug out the phone book yellow pages. YEP...there it was...a big ad...so I tore it out.

Jackson is a pretty good sized town, and my walking covered about 1/8th of it, if that much. Those "folks up there" know just how to plant those directions in your mind!! I remember Larry telling me that this type of "sub-conscious planting" goes on constantly with him. These spirits are getting to be more fun all the time.

Journal Discussion: August 22, 2001

It is now time to take stock of the last six months.

Evaluation of the past events, where are we now, and what can we do to proceed to bigger and better things. That means...developing to a higher level.

1) Evaluation: Mostly, very unusual "coincidences" have been the main theme. But Patty's visits have to top the list, because we know now that spirits can actually visit us right in our house, and we must assume that they can again. <u>We are asking for more.</u> Secondly, it would have to be the "near accident" that Patty experienced. (However, I am still not sure how they put that cloud over Lebanon, though.)

We are convinced that they can manipulate electricity...there just have been too many weird things happening to our TV and appliances. And NONE of their tricks have been damaging or more than very temporary. We never had those things happen before and no event has happened twice. They started soon after we began our meditations and opened ourselves to the spiritual dimension, being convinced now that it does exist. And....we have to assume that if they can get into the house and appear as a body, then fooling with electricity must be a cinch. (I am wondering if they have to go to school and get a license to be fooling with the electricity. Also, they pay no attention whatsoever to burglar alarms.)

The chance meeting with Larry Hastings was a really BIG plus.... he has confirmed all that I have read, and now I have a real person to call when I have questions.

We are convinced that spirits can "implant" thoughts in our sub-conscious or even our conscious mind. This leads to some of the coincidences. We are also convinced that they are aware of our activities (if they want to be), and they can communicate through dreams or receive communications through meditation or prayer.

I think my daughter is okay because the signs came back pretty fast. If it wasn't her sending them, it could have been her guardian spirit or mine. In either case, this is very comforting. I was not looking for those signs...and in truth...I thought I was spinning my wheels. But they showed up when I was least expecting them. And either the same day or within a couple days later.

2) Where we are now: It is often very frustrating to know that mediums like John Edward can hear these folks, and I can't. I am still working on that. But at least I now believe it is possible. I want to know if this gift must be "inborn" or can it be developed. Cause if it is inborn, then I am wasting my time in meditation. I might as well just ask them to booger the TV again.

Same with OBE's. Very often my meditations are aimed toward an out-of-body experience, but so far...nothing. Although I think I am getting closer. I am able to numb my body so that I can't feel it, and during the last try I even felt it "vibrating." But it is still frustrating...like you taxied out to the runway for take-off, but the tower won't clear you.

There is no question that these experiences have gotten our full attention, and our studies in this area are slowly changing our lives and the way we perceive reality and God and humankind. And it is all for the better. This "hobby" is filled with nothing but love for all and a stronger belief in God.

We want more. The more you learn, the more you want. It is addictive. Patty and I were never very religious, because we just couldn't see how ...with all these religions, only one was right, or more right, like many of them preach. And to think of the millions of people who died in religious wars, what a waste. But now...we have a belief system that makes a lot of sense, and the best part is...there are more and more indications that it is very real, and that we *can* take an active part in it.

3) Developing a higher level: John Edward and other mediums say we *can* develop our perceptive or psychic powers more fully...that it is there, and you just have to tap it. It can be achieved through meditation, prayer, and a strong belief that the

spirit dimension does exist. I wish he said you could advance faster after a few martinis, but I tried that several times and it doesn't work. Wouldn't ya know there is no easy way.

So...I am now working toward: more coincidences; achieving an OBE; more vivid dreams; more visual spirit visits; trying to find out who my spirit guide is, and communicating like John does. Lotsa luck, but at least it is fun trying. And I feel much better about things.... like being better connected to higher levels than just this screwed-up place called Earth. And I am certainly no longer afraid of that situation we call "death", since there really is no death. You just cross over to the other side. Okay!! Let's get on with it. What's next, guys???

Chapter 4

Strategies and
Tactics

Journal Discussion: Tuesday, August 28 to Saturday, Sept 1, 2001

Not much is happening lately. Our thinking is this: we asked them for signs that they exist, and they gave us plenty; I asked three times for a sign from Laurie, and they gave me all three; I asked to meet a person with an NDE, they came through; we <u>didn't</u> ask for a real "visit", but someone from the spirit dimension threw that in as a bonus. Plus....add a "feeling" implanted in Patty's mind that avoided an auto accident.

I know what Larry would tell me...that they are saying: "Hey now...we have other things to do up here....so cool it for awhile."

Therefore we have to try a different strategy. They won't come to us? Let's go to their world!

We decided to try and find a legitimate medium in Dallas. Yeah, right. I'm sure the yellow pages are full of them. (They were, but I don't think so!")

I went Suzane Northrop's web site theseance.com, which was mentioned in her book. There was a message board there. I posted a message, asking if anyone knew a legitimate medium in the Dallas area. Two days later this arrived in my email:

FROM: *Jill Christopher-Moore*

DATE: *Thursday, August 30, 2001 5:26 PM*

> *Bob, Shannon Maxey (www.inquirewithin.net) works primarily with grief counseling, but can refer you if you are "just curious". She does spirit communication with those in grief. She seemed to be quite good to me......Jill*

I sent an email to Shannon. She sent back a long email reply the next day. A week later, she called me and we set up an appointment for <u>October 3, 2001 at 2 pm.</u> She said it was $85 for Patty and me, but if we didn't like the reading, there was no charge. Now THAT is my kind of reading!

And October 3rd happens to be one day after Laurie's birthday.

<u>Journal Discussion: September 1, 2001 to September 20, 2001</u>

No new visits...no more electrical quirks. So, I am working on meditation and trying to learn how to experience an OBE. Reading three books on OBE's, and how to trigger them. But it is a very long process learning this stuff.

One thing I have noticed though. Since I started doing meditations (which include meditations for health), my blood pressure has steadily gone down. I have no other explanation for it. On my last few pilot physicals, I had to cut the coffee that morning to keep my bp within limits, because I have always been about 150-170 over 95-100. Sometimes the doc had to take it twice after I lay down a bit, just to get it below 140 / 90.

On the last physical (Sep 18)...including coffee...it was 124 over 74. The doc asked me how I did that. I just said I don't know (because I am certainly not going to tell him "that the dead folks are helping me".)

But I wasn't concerned any more, because it has been low like this for the last 3 months. I am beginning to wonder if meditation has other benefits also. It reminds me a lot of self-hypnosis. John's tapes indicate that meditation can help keep you healthy in body, mind, spirit and attitude. I will pursue that more.

Journal Entry: Early September 2001

I came upon a very interesting article. **Professors at the University of Arizona** were doing scientific testing on well-known mediums, including John Edward, George Anderson, and Suzane Northrop. Here is the article:

Study finds psychics can commune with the dead.

Robert Matthews, The Sunday Telegraph - A series of experiments at the University of Arizona has produced evidence that researchers say could indicate that some "mediums" might indeed be able to communicate with the dead.

Most mainstream scientists dismiss the entire realm of paranormal abilities as the domain of the deluded and the fraudulent. However, Gary Schwartz, a professor of psychology at the university's Tucson campus, took the question seriously enough to lead a laboratory study of mediums: people who claim to be able to commune with the dead.

He said the findings suggest the mediums studied seemed to possess an uncanny ability to state facts about the deceased relatives of complete strangers, with as much as 93% accuracy. "The bottom line is that there is a class of highly skilled mediums who are doing something extraordinary," said Mr. Schwartz. His findings are to be published this week in the Journal of the Society for Psychical Research.

In the experiments, conducted at the university's Human Energy Systems Laboratory, five mediums were asked to contact the departed relatives of two people who were not known to them. In the first experiment, each medium spent an hour with a subject in a laboratory, with a screen preventing them from getting visual clues. Under constant video surveillance, each began talking about the subject's deceased relatives.

The subjects were allowed to respond to specific questions from the medium, but only with a "yes" or "no." At the end of each session, the information gleaned by the mediums was analyzed for its accuracy. The transcripts of each session showed that the mediums typically produced more than 80 pieces of information about the deceased, from names and personal idiosyncrasies to the circumstances of their death.

Mr. Schwartz said that when he analyzed the factual accuracy of the mediums' information, they achieved a success rate of 83%, with a high score of 93%. Similar success was achieved when the experiment was conducted with the second subject, and even when the mediums were not allowed to communicate directly with the subject.

The Arizona researchers said they asked a panel of more than 60 non-mediums to supply the same information as the mediums about the same subjects. Their average score was only 36%, with the most successful guesser achieving just 54%.

And Mr. Schwartz said he took every precaution to rule out unconscious cheating or outright fraud.

They came out with a report, and also an email address to obtain a copy. I wrote an email to Gary Schwartz and he sent back a copy of the entire report. However...I wanted a little more than just the report, so I wrote to Professor Schwartz personally.

September 26, 2001

Dear Gary:

A month ago you were kind enough to send me this report on mediums. Again, I thank you. I have been following John Edward and George Anderson for over a year.

Now... this new request may be a little off base, but I won't know unless I ask.

Disregarding all the "scientific" data you gathered for the report, and aside from the investigation...and after knowing the results...could you please tell me what your personal thoughts are concerning the validity of these mediums?

Had the experiments changed your belief in any way?

I promise I won't tell Connie Chung.

Thank you......Bob Dean

And I got the following replies.

FROM GARY: September 25, 2001

Hi - my personal reaction is simple. I know, as a fact, that in our laboratory, people like Laurie Campbell, John Edward, George Anderson, and others, are doing something VERY REAL. How much of it is mind reading of the living and mind reading of the dead, that is a complex question. My overall impression is that the data requires an interpretation of survival of consciousness. A curious conclusion from someone well trained to be a devout agnostic.

Hope this helps......Warmly, Gary

FROM GARY: September 26, 2001

Hi - thanks for the very informative email. Yes, there are a few genuine mediums...they are doing something...and I do not think it is all mind reading of the physically living. This winter my book *THE AFTERLIFE EXPERIMENTS; BREAKTHROUGH SCIENTIFIC EVIDENCE OF LIFE AFTER DEATH* (Schwartz with Simon, Pocket Books) will be published. Detailed studies are reviewed there. Good luck with your adventure in this area...Zammit's site is amazing...I have not had time to read his book......Warmly, Gary

Journal Note: Gary's book came out in December, and I now have it in my library. The information in that book merely added more credibility to my own conclusions, but now I have enhanced that credibility from an unbiased, scientific point of view.

Journal Entry: September 30 - October 2, 2001

Preparation for the Medium.

In preparation for the visit to Shannon Maxey, Patty and I tried to get in tune for a couple of days in advance....just as Shannon had requested. This meant thinking and meditating about all those who we wanted to come through.

Of course, my daughter Laurie was on the top of my list, followed by my Viet Nam roommate Stan Cox, who was killed in action; my own father, who died of alcoholism when I was in high school; my old high school buddy and very close friend David Stevens, who was killed in Naval jet training back in 1957.

Patty's thoughts were aimed at her father and her uncle Jack, with whom she was very close; Mary Helen Bifano and Betty Heidenrich, older ladies and two of her previous work-related good friends.

(Patty believes that these two ladies were the spirits who visited her with the roses. She knew Mary Helen a lot longer than Betty, hence the difference in the number of roses.)

Journal Entry: Wednesday, October 3, 2001

A medium kind of day.

Our appointment with medium Shannon Maxey was at 2:00 pm in Arlington, Texas, about an hour from our house. Patty took the afternoon off from work.

Now I have no doubt anymore about the abilities of John Edward or George Anderson or Suzane Northrop, but being a skeptic in the basic sense, I was not expecting to be wowed like a patron in John's Gallery, even though someone else recommended this medium. Patty was more confident of this adventure.

Shannon was pleasant. She explained how the reading worked for 30 minutes, and then she took a 20-minute break to meditate, while we took a break in another room. Then the reading began, and it was being taped for us to take home.

Shannon was pretty general in some areas, but there were a few definite "hits" which would seem to validate her abilities. What made the reading more difficult was the fact that Patty's family and my family were both coming through, and it was sometimes difficult to determine which side was making a reference.

Here is a brief summary of important inputs with my comments included. This is taken from the tape that we still have. Shannon's part is in bold.

The Reading

The first energy I'm getting is an older male for Patty...on your dad's side. Does May or the 5th of a month have a meaning?

Patty: Daddy was born in May.

He also has his brother with him.

Patty: My uncle, who I was close to, has also passed.

(Note: We did not tell her any of this...there is no way she could have known of Patty's uncle who had crossed over.)

Oh, Bob he's got your daughter with him. There is a daughter figure in the spirit with him.

Your family and Bob's family all come together.

Where's August or the 8th of a month?

Patty: I was born in August.

Bob: There's more for August. My daughter passed away in August.

She has a male friend of yours, Bob who has crossed either in Viet Nam or because of Viet Nam. His crossing was before hers and he met her when she crossed over.

Bob: My friend.

(NOTE: This was exactly right on. She did not know of Stan.)

Is there a meaning for 18? Or the 18th of a month?

Patty: Daddy died on Jan. 18

Why is October important?

Bob: My daughter's birthday was yesterday, October 2.

She's thanking you for continuing to celebrate her life. She is glad you haven't forgotten about her. That you celebrate her life and not dwell on the events leading to her passing. She

says you talk to her regularly. She likes flying with you. She flies with you regularly. She says she is an angel on your wings...like a guardian angel on your wings.

She thanks you Bob for what you buried with her. You...Bob...put something in her casket. She saw that and thanks you for that.

(Note: I did put one of her favorite paintings in the casket....that her mother and I agreed upon. This was kind of a surprise. No way she could know that.)

And there is a story behind this, also. In Laurie's room, she had an arrangement of 8 or 9 of her best paintings and hung them on the wall. Karen, her mother, and I had already decided to put one of the paintings in the casket, but we had not decided which one. When we went into Laurie's room to decide, one of the paintings was missing. I asked Karen if she already took it, and she said no.

After a few minutes of being totally baffled, we looked in back of the cabinet that was under the paintings, and there was the missing one. It had just fallen down behind the cabinet "by itself".

Karen and I just looked at each other, and we came to the conclusion that Laurie had already made the choice for us. And I **did** put that painting into the casket.

You all must have had a terrific relationship and a close bond with lots of understanding. She said you were her protector but you could not have foreseen her passing. She doesn't want you to feel any responsibility for her passing. She says you still bear responsibility and she says to let that

go. It is not right. She says she has a good relationship with your father. Apparently there was no time or contact with him in her life.

Bob: My father passed a couple years before Laurie was born.

(There was no way she could have known that.)

Where's Lisa or Elisa?

Patty: Bob's niece.

Your daughter is acknowledging Lisa or Elisa. And your daughter calls out to Mom. Mom must be living?

Bob: Yes.

<<Skipping >>

Is there any reason why your daughter would keep wanting to say hello to Elisa?

Bob: Not anymore than anyone else.

(Note added Nov 2003: yes….there was!!! A future event.)

Patty...your dad is acknowledging the 23rd. Dad is also acknowledging a new addition or additions to the family on your kids side Patty.

Patty: The grandkids.

Your daughter is mentioning…that you have a brother living Bob?

Bob: Yes…my brother Ronnie

And where's the Catholic stuff?

Bob: The only thing I can think of is…my nieces Elisa and Holly were initially brought up Catholic.

Where's the CA - Catharine or Carol or Carolyn?

Patty: My two sisters - Kathy and Carolyn.

(Note: Very interesting that she got both of Patty's sisters' names correctly…we had NOT at all mentioned them.)

Dad says 'hello to them'. Elizabeth - I was seeing Beth but then they lengthened it to Elizabeth.

Patty: Daddy's mother's name was Elizabeth.

Your daughter also says someone dealt with or is dealing with an alcohol issue? She mentioned it and I said I don't want to talk about it but she insisted I bring it up.

Bob: My Dad died of alcohol.

(Note: Later…Patty said I was avoiding the issue…and that I knew full well what she was getting at. Well…I do sometimes have too many martinis before dinner. Leave it to Laurie to side with Patty.)

I'm getting an ST --- Stephen? Scott?

Patty: Stan maybe…Bob's roommate in Viet Nam who was killed.

(To Patty...) Besides Tammy...your daughter's name... I am getting Terry?

Patty: My kid's dad...my first husband.

Good thing he's your ex. Dad is saying that's for the best. Was dad alive when you divorced?

Patty: No.

Was he of the belief that once you get married; you stay married?

Patty: Definitely.

Cassidy? (to Bob) **Does the name Cassidy mean anything?**

Bob: Not that I know of.

(Note: Later, I realized that it probably referred to Hopalong Cassidy. Bill Sumrall...an email friend and old Braniff buddy, and I were joking about him watching old Hopalong Cassidy movies on TV, and we joked and made puns for a week about that...the previous week. I guess this was Laurie's way of telling me that she is around and often sees what we are doing.)

And I'm getting R for you Patty? Or Ruth?

Patty: Mom's middle name.

Mom and dad must have had a deep devotion and commitment? She has not remarried?

Patty: No

He understands but said it would be ok; even though that would seem like a different attitude than other people would think of him. He says sometimes she is lonely but 'you girls' ....Did he refer to you and your sisters as 'you girls'?

Patty: Yes. He would always say "YOU GIRLS COME HERE!! Or...YOU GIRLS ARE GONNA BE THE DEATH OF ME!!

He is thanking you all for helping mom and supporting her and letting her know her family hasn't abandoned her. He says you all still make her very much a part of the family and he is thanking you for that. He is mentioning the Aquarius connection again?

Patty: Mom's sister's birthday.

Does she have some mobility problems?

Patty: She has arthritis.

Has where she lives been adjusted because of that?

Patty: Yes...She was living in an upstairs apartment but moved to a ground level apartment.

He seems to have a real desire to want to take care of her. He likes Bob. Bob and your dad must have had similar qualities?

Patty: Yes.

    Journal Summary: One of the things I need to emphasize here is that Laurie came through pretty strong, and said that I need to become closer to my other two daughters and to the whole family. It was almost like she was going to "help that along".

(Added note from the future: Little did I know how the coming events would shortly unfold right according to Laurie's plan.)

Journal Entry: Friday, October 5, 2001

Am I being set up here???

I listened to the tape again, and I have not been able to figure out who "Beth" is. I was not convinced that it was on Patty's side of the family. When Laurie died, I was on an airline trip. Laurie was at home fooling with her car in the garage, and a friend of hers was in the house. Was that Beth? I couldn't remember, and it started to bug me.

I called my mother in Atlanta to see if she remembered, but she could not. Then I thought of calling my daughter Sheri, but I did not want her to know why I was asking such a weird question.

Well...it finally bugged me so much that I called Sheri on Friday night and asked, "Sheri...do you remember the name of the friend who was with Laurie when she died?"

There was a moment of silence, then Sheri asked, "Dad...why are you asking me this?"

I said, "Just answer the question." But she refused, unless I explained why. So...I had to explain about our visit to the medium. To my complete surprise, Sheri came back with, "Sit down, Dad...this phone call is going to last a few hours."

Then Sheri proceeded to tell me about her "visit" from Laurie, and how she had "out-of-body" experiences, and how she was told by a friend to read George Anderson's book in order to understand OBE's and visits from the afterlife. I was totally stunned by this "awakening"...my **own daughter.** And she was afraid to tell *me*, just as I was afraid to tell *her.*

Yes, Laurie did...in her unique way...bring Sheri and I closer together, and now we visit more and have long phone calls about the afterlife, Laurie, OBE's, and after death communications.

(NOTE: More of Sheri's story in the appendix.)

Journal Entry: October 10, 2001

They're baaaack...Patty's Story.

It was just after 9:00 pm, and Bob was on a trip. I was watching one of my favorite shows, Sex and the City, when all of a sudden the TV went silent and the screen became filled with a beautiful lime-green color. (Lime-green is my favorite color.)

I tried to turn the TV off, but it would not turn off. I switched to another channel, but it too was lime-green. After about three minutes, and after I yelled something like "Cut the crap you guys...I'm watching a show!!" The TV came back to normal all by itself with the show in progress. It had never done that before, and had not done it since.

I know who is doing it, so I just take it in stride and thank them again for letting me know they are hanging around.

Journal Entry: November 15, 2001 The Bill Sumrall Story

Background info: Bill Sumrall is a good friend of mine who lives in Howe, Texas. We were old Braniff pilots together, and he retired when Braniff went bankrupt in 1989. We remained good friends, meeting on occasion and in the last 5 years by email and telephone.

Bill and I usually agreed on politics, but when it came to the "afterlife", Bill's attitude was, "Bob, when your dead, you're dead. There IS NO AFTERLIFE!!! There is no God!!"

Well...Bill and I went back and forth on this for six months after I got into John Edward. I got him to watch JE a couple times, but then he said "This is a bunch of crap. He's a fake. You've got to be naïve if you think dead people can communicate with us!"

Often I would kid him saying things like, "When I cross over Bill, I am gonna come back and bugger your computer." His answer was, "Well...if something happens to ME PERSONALLY, then I'll believe it."

During some of my meditations, I even asked "the boys" to visit Mister Bill. Jan, his wife, was not as much of a skeptic as Bill, but that didn't phase Bill one bit.

Now...the day of reckoning.

This is his email on November 15 (and the follow-up on Dec 7, 2001):

<u>Received Thursday, November 15, 2001 From Bill Sumrall.</u>

Bob...Jan said I was obligated to send you this...don't give me any crap. But it is true, and I admit...I have no explanation. Jan's mom died Oct. 31st. Buried in Mississippi on 2 Nov. around 11AM. At 1PM, and for about 20 minutes, we were packing the car from motel room for trip home.

Around 3PM and 100 miles down the road I look at the cell phone. It has one voice-mail message waiting. I picked up the phone and took the message...it was just music and not knowing how long some prankster might have the phone tied up, I hung up.

At 5 PM the phone rang again with a voice-message. I picked up and it was the same message sent at the same time, 1:07 PM (while we were loading car). I let Jan listen and it was organ funeral music! It played for 2 minutes. At the conclusion the message was cleared from the phone.

The next morning at 8AM the phone rang, it was the same voice-message recorded at 1:07PM previous day - which we had listened to twice and cleared the message each time. Then again at 5PM phone rang, same message which was again recorded at 1:07PM on the previous day.

Since then there had been no more weird messages. Another oddity is that the 'caller ID' said the call was coming from my cell phone number, which would be impossible to call myself on my own cell phone.

I re-read my phone manual 3 times and could never explain it. Jan said it was a message from her mom saying there was a hereafter! Another thing, there was no music at the funeral!

Sum....

Friday, December 7, 2001 follow-up email from Bill.

Received cell phone statement today. **Not one of the 6 calls is listed!**

Sum...

I wrote back to him, "Of course not, Bill. They don't go through our phone system, LOL."

Well...Bill has since "revised" his thinking a bit, and is now somewhat open to the afterlife.

Journal Entry: Friday, December 21 to Monday, December 24, 2001

Preliminary information: On a bookcase shelf in my office is an 8 x 10 framed picture of the Lear jet and the two of us pilots leaning on the nose section, taken two years ago when I first worked for the company. The heavy frame has a regular flap-tab on the back so that the picture leans back about 45 degrees and stands by itself.

On Friday, December 21, I had a trip to Lebanon, Missouri...again. A layover for four days, with nothing to do. (Except perhaps see Larry for a few hours, if he is home.)

The bosses have property there, and it appears that this type of trip will become routine for all of the year 2002 ...and that means I will be gone for most all of my weekends and holidays for the foreseeable future. (Also...my night vision depth perception is getting worse, and that is not good for a pilot.)

I am becoming more and more inclined to retire from the company and perhaps become an independent contract pilot, but the decision is a very difficult one to make, since it is a good job in most all other ways. I also need to consider the probability of a drop in income and benefits. This dilemma began to bear on my mind all day Friday.

On Saturday morning, Larry came to the hotel for a chat, and we talked about "the boys" again, and he reiterated how they just keep him going on the right track...using the most unusual methods.

I have not been meditating for awhile, and since the hotel was quiet in Lebanon, I decided to talk to the boys again. Saturday night I began meditation before falling asleep. The main topic...I asked for some help in making a decision to retire. Sunday afternoon I tried again, and Sunday night before falling asleep, "C'mon guys...I need some help here."

On Monday, we were due to leave for Dallas at 3 pm. At twelve noon, I called Patty and told her. As we talked, she said something a little out of the ordinary like, "be very careful on this trip."

When she repeated that again at the end of the conversation, I asked her why is she saying that. She said, "I will tell you when you get home."

The trip was routine. Arriving home about 4 pm, I asked her what was the concern.

Here is Patty's story:

Patty: I was in the kitchen at about 9:30 am when I heard a loud "bang" in the office area. I thought that some Christmas gift or roll of paper had fallen down in the hall closet, so I went to check. Nothing there had fallen. So...I went to the office, and the picture of Bob and Buron with the Lear had fallen over FACE DOWN!

Now there is absolutely no possible way it could do that, because it was leaning backwards like all pictures do...and in fact about 45 degrees backwards. This scared me tremendously, since my first thought was that Bob and Buron were going to crash or have some big kind of problem with the jet. There was absolutely no doubt as to who did this...but I couldn't figure out WHY they did it.

Then Bob laughed and laughed...he said, "That is the sign!! They are telling me it is okay to retire from the flying! I meditated on that in Lebanon. I thought they ignored me."

Patty said, "Why didn't you tell me that? I thought it was something bad about to happen."

I said, "Because they were supposed to answer me, not you...(laughing)."

This is certainly a milestone in our connections with the folks, because it is the first time they have actually moved a solid object. And we both repeat...there was no possible way that picture could have fallen forward. There was no fan on, no air movement, no window open, nothing of this earth could have caused that. They have boogered the TV before, and the VCR and the cell phone and the clock, but they have never before actually moved anything physically. Amazing!!

The fact that the picture fell forward...well...I took it as a sign that it is okay now to retire from the job they had given me over two years ago. And that all will be okay. We all have free will on this earth, so I still have to make the decision myself but at least they say it is alright...that it is an okay move.

✳ *Part Two* ✳
Addressing the questions and drawing a road map.

Chapter 5 If You Build it, They Will Come

Journal Discussion: January, 2002

As I look back to reflect the events of the years 2000 and 2001, I see that period as an important turning point for my belief system and spiritual attitudes. I went from a total skeptic to a confirmed believer. As a skeptic, I could always say that many of the events were "coincidences," but they just kept happening more and more, and there was no way I could get around that. As John says...the folks up there often take an active part in your lives through what you "think" are coincidences.

The fact that Patty and I began to feel the effects reminds me of the movie *"Field of Dreams"* where he said, "If you build it, they will come." You have to build a receptive mindset and that takes time, patience, practice, meditation, and a confirmed belief. But...if you build it...they will come.

Looking back has also brought more questions. What was the "Beth" name for? Why did the medium keep referring to my niece Elisa? How do tragedies like the World Trade Center enter into the scheme of things? Why can't I receive clairaudience signals like mediums do?

I learned that our fate is pretty much determined before we are even born on this earth, and that strange events can occur in our lives to help us understand this. As I personally look back on events in my life, I realize more and more that this is a given. I can now understand more fully why I was spared in Viet Nam, and my roommate died. Here is Stan's story.

Back to the past...1967

I was a captain in the US Air Force, stationed with the 315th Air Commando Squadron in Nha Trang, Viet Nam. I flew a C-123 cargo plane, and our main job was to supply the little Special Forces bases all over the country, either by landing or by parachute. (Sometimes we hauled more Playboy magazines and San Miguel beer than ammunition.)

But we had another mission, which no one particularly liked...night flare drop missions. If a Green Beret base was being attacked at night, our job was to fly orbit over the base and drop flares, which usually stopped the attack. It was on one of these missions that the Green Berets, who we protected during a bad thunderstorm, put my whole crew in for the Distinguished Flying Cross...the highest honor in the Air Force.

Five of us officers lived in a villa in Nha Trang. My roommate and best friend there was also a captain named Stan Cox. Stan was safety officer for our squadron. Once a week, we were on "Flare Duty." My night was Thursday. Stan's night was Wednesday.

But...Stan had a safety meeting on one particular Wednesday, and he asked me to switch nights with him. If we were called to a mission, he would take my crew on Thursday.

On Wednesday night I was not called for any mission. On Thursday night, Stan *was* called out with my crew. The next morning, the Colonel came to visit me, and said, "I am sorry to report to you that Captain Stanley Cox and your crew were shot down on their mission last night, and they are all confirmed dead."

Go figure. I was in charge of taking care of his things, an experience I will never forget.

If you ever see a list of folks killed in Viet Nam (like at the memorial in DC)..look for Stan Cox. He's there...it was almost me.

As I look back, for 30 years I figured I was just lucky. But...knowing what I know now, I believe it was just not my time.

Another related story unfolds when I called Larry last month. I often call him when I have some questions that I can't resolve. I wanted to know how "fate" deals with tragedies like the World Trade Center.

When I called Larry today about the WTC question, he said, "Didn't I tell you about my son Mark?" I said no, I don't think so.

Larry's Story (Larry is still a KingAir pilot for a furniture company in Lebanon.)

Larry has a son, 34 years old, named Mark. Mark is an investment banker. He works with other financiers all over the United States. Mark had an office in the WTC with Morgan-Stanley until about March 2001. For some "reason" Mark wanted to move his office, so he left the WTC then, apparently to somewhere near Boston. But his connections were still all over the US, and still with Morgan-Stanley at the WTC.

(I asked Larry at this point was his son "psychic" in any way. Larry said his son would never go into that, but Larry always thought he was "sensitive" to things.)

Mark had a business appointment with Morgan-Stanley on the morning of Sept 11, 2001 at the WTC offices. But....a day or two before that, some big wig from Los Angeles called Mark with a billion dollar deal they were putting together, and needed him there right away. So, Mark called Morgan-Stanley and re-scheduled the appointment at the WTC offices and booked a non-stop flight from Boston to LA on Sept 11...on the famous Flight 175!!

Hang on.... it gets better!!!!

The night of Sept 10, the big wig from LA called and said they had delayed the deal because of snags, and to cancel the trip, which he did. Since Mark had already re-scheduled the WTC appointment, he did not go there on Sept 11.

WAIT.... there's more!!!

A business friend of Mark's worked for Morgan-Stanley. That friend was never late for his job. But on the morning of Sept 11, he overslept!!! And so he decided to take the morning off as a personal half day. Go figure.

Larry thinks that all those who died there...it was their time. And many, many who were scheduled to be there on that morning were either not at the office yet, or were diverted...because it was NOT their time.

But Larry also admits...he is not certain about all this pre-destiny stuff...he just tries to work with what he has learned from Joshua.

Journal Entry: February 2002

My daughter Sheri was quite intrigued about my reading with Shannon Maxey last October 3rd. So, she decided to get an appointment with Shannon.

Background Information...Sheri's Story:

About a year ago, on February 28th, 2001, a friend and co-worker of mine named Vickie was involved in a terrible car accident while going to a teen revival meeting. Vickie's husband was in intensive care for two months, and while she and her son survived the accident with minor injuries, her 12-year-old daughter Jessica was killed.

Since I had experienced my sister's death (Laurie), I had some understanding of the pain Vickie was going through. I told her she could talk or cry with me at any time, and I went with her to see her husband in ICU almost every day. Needless to say, Vickie and I became much closer.

Vickie has a very strong faith in God. She was incredibly strong during the whole ordeal. In January of 2002, my Dad gave me the name of a medium in Dallas named Shannon Maxey. I wanted Vickie to go with me, but she was uncomfortable about that. She did, however, support me in going.

During my reading with Shannon, I was focusing on "hearing" from my own family and from Vickie's daughter Jessica. I got confused many times during the reading, because Shannon was asking what I thought were questions about Vickie's family, which I did not know in depth.

However, Shannon kept asking if Jessica had a friend named "Megan." (Like…Jessica kept wanting to say hello to a Megan). I told her that I didn't know for sure, but I would ask. Later that night, I brought Vickie to my house and played her the tape. She could not figure out who Megan was either. So we just kind of dropped it there, like there must have been some mistake.

Sheri's Journal Entry…April 2002

Vickie's sister-in-law goes to a teen revival…the same revival that Jessica was planning to attend when she was killed. A young girl at the revival approached her and began talking about Jessica. The girl told her that she was a good friend of Jessica and that she missed Jessica very much. She went on to explain how they had traded lockers at school and how the school accidentally took her things out of the locker thinking that they were Jessica's things. She had to get that straightened out.

Then….Vickie's sister-in-law asked her who she was. She said, "My name is Megan."

Vickie came to me the next day, and told me the story. I was totally wide-eyed. I said to Vickie, "You know what this means, don't you? That it WAS Jessica talking through Shannon! No one else could know this!" We were both astounded.

Journal Entry: June 26, 2002...Re-visiting Bill Sumrall's cell phone call

Email to Bill:

Hey Bill...I was adding some notes to my afterlife journal this morning, and re-read your story about the cell phone calls. Now I am curious again, and decided to ask you a few questions.

Those calls...are there any other possibilities of how they were made to your phone? Are you totally convinced they were a last good-bye from Jan's mother?

Bill's Reply:

Bob...here's what occurred:

Her mom was buried the morning of November 2nd. That afternoon while loading the car and checking out of the motel, we received a voice-mail at 1:07 PM (we were loading and checking out from 1:00 PM until 1:20 PM). We weren't in the car and did not hear the phone ring. Later, about 1:45 PM while driving home, I noticed that the voice-mail icon was on so I listened to it (it was the 1:07 PM call we had missed). However, there was no talking, just organ music so I hung up right away thinking it was a wrong number or crank call.

(Note: There was no music at the funeral.)

Few people have our cell phone number anyway. So at 1:49 PM we called Jan's cousin who was enroute back to Cary, North Carolina, to ask if they made the 'crank' call. (The invoice says we called Cary, but that is their cell phone base). They didn't answer so I left a voice-mail asking if they had called. At 3:57

PM they returned my call (on the invoice) and said they had not. For the next 2 days there is no record of an incoming call of any kind.

At 5:00 PM the same day the phone rings. Says I have a voice-mail. It was organ music again. Since I did not listen to the entire message the first time, I figured it was not automatically erased so I handed the phone to Jan and asked her to let the message run its course so we could erase it. Organ music played for 2 minutes, then quit. I thought I erased it, but not positive.

Day #2:

Phone rang as we were having breakfast at 8:00 AM. Said we had voice-mail. We listened. Same organ music, same length of time. This time I made sure I erased it. At 5:00 PM, suppertime, phone rang, said we had voice-mail. Listened to same music, same length of time. Had read and re-read my cell phone manual and was erasing message correctly. So, erased it again.

Day #3:

At 7:15AM, again at breakfast, phone rang and said we had voice-mail. Listened to same as above again and erased again. At 5:00 PM phone rang and said we had voice-mail. Same-o, same-o. Erased again.

Day #4:

Early morning, Jan came running in and said she just thought that it must be her mom trying to convey life after death. **Her having said that, we have received no more such calls.**

In the meantime I would look at the caller ID on the phone to see who placed the call. Each time it had our own cell phone number. I told Jan, we'd catch the perpetrators when the phone bill arrived as it lists each incoming and outgoing call. There was no incoming calls at all for that period - nothing other than the one call from her cousin returning our call.

Yes...Jan watches *Crossing Over* every day now. I am still buffaloed.

....Bill Sum

Journal Entry: August 15, 2002

Here is another little story about being "connected." Personally, I think Patty is more connected to the folks than I am and she has even better stories than I do. She has actually had a materialized visit...and I never have. I just see or feel their effects.

I retired from my corporate flying job last March, and told the chief pilot that I would fly for them on a "contract pilot" basis, if they needed someone. Nothing came up so far.

Okay...it is the beginning of July, 2002, and Patty wants a vacation. I asked where and she said she would like to go to Las Vegas one last time, and the package prices were pretty cheap. (Well...I didn't think so, and you have to go by airline...UGH!.) She finds this contest, where the winner gets 3 days in Vegas. She enters the contest and tells me that her spirit guides will help her win. She is always pulling this stuff on me. I said laughing, "Well...make sure your guides don't make us fly on an airline."

So...the "contest" means we have to go 120 miles away to visit some new property estates, right? HA!!! I sat around all day trying to figure out how to get out of that little deal. Meanwhile, Patty is still talking to her spirit guide.

On July 20th, Buron, the Chief pilot calls me and says, "Bob...I cannot make a company trip on August 10 to August 13...do you want to take it ?"

I said "Sure...where's it go?"

He says, "Just fly to Las Vegas...stay for 3 days...and come back. We'll pay you $1200. You will be staying at the Luxor. And...(this is very rare, folks)...there are just 3 ladies going, so the boss says both you pilots can take your wives."

Well it took me about minus 3 seconds to answer THAT really tough question. When I told Patty....she just laughs, and says, "You need to fire ole George Burns and get you a WOMAN spirit guide....ha ha ha."

So...we had a great time...all expenses paid vacation. There is no question in my mind why this came about. Or...who did it.

Coincidence? I don't think so. Connections? ...For sure.

Journal Entry: September 8, 2002 ...Elisa's Story

Background: My brother (Ronnie) and sister-in-law (Mary Ann) live in Roswell, Georgia, a suburb of Atlanta. They have two grown daughters living near them, Elisa (or Lisa) and Holly. Elisa is married. She and her husband had been trying hard to have a child, but after 3 miscarriages, they were about to give up. However...Elisa became pregnant (one last time) in February of 2002. As of June, Lisa's pregnancy was normal, and going better than the previous times.

We were never really close to Ronnie's side of the family because of the distance involved...but we had a family reunion every five years or so. We did, on occasion, send jokes out to each other on email.

The Georgia folks decided to have a family reunion on July 4-6 at our place in Dallas. My two daughters, Lynda and Sheri, would also be here with their husbands. Lisa got permission from her doctor to travel to Dallas, since she had several months to go, and so far...no complications.

Everyone arrived on July 4th and 5th, and had hotel rooms near us. Elisa and Rusty used our guest room. On July 5th, Rusty and Elisa were visiting some other relatives in Denison, Texas, and Elisa had stomach pains. They went to the nearest hospital, and were immediately ambulanced to Baylor Hospital in Dallas....probably the best facility in the US for preemie births. Lisa was immediately hospitalized.

She spent 19 days there, and the decision was made by Dr. Andersen (this Dr. has been on The Learning Channel many times, and is an expert on preemies) to have the baby. It would be 3 months early. Little Collin James was born on July 21, at 1 pound and 8 ounces. He was no bigger than your hand. Of course, he was living on tubes and in intensive care, and it was touch-and-go every day.

Elisa went to see and feed the little guy every day for several hours. But she would sometimes come home in tears because the doctor said CJ had something wrong with his eyes...or his lungs...or some other complications.

I tried to console her as best I could, and Patty and I had our angels watching over CJ. Even the angel on the ceiling came over every day, as if to say, "I'm watching...it will be okay." When I meditated, I began to plead "Hey guys...I really need some help here!!"

Well, the folks answered again, as they always do, in their wonderful little ways. This time it was an email going around that I received in early August from a Canadian internet friend, GeoBear. The email was apparently written several years ago.

The email: The Smell of Rain

A cold March wind danced around the dead of night in Dallas as the Doctor walked into the small hospital room of Diana Blessing. Still groggy from surgery, her husband David held her hand as they braced themselves for the latest news. That afternoon of March 10, 1991, complications had forced Diana, only 24 weeks pregnant, to deliver Danae Lu Blessing.

At 12 inches long and weighing only one pound and nine ounces, they already knew she was perilously premature. Still, the doctor's soft words dropped like bombs. I don't think she's going to make it, he said, as kindly as he could. "There's only a 10 percent chance she will live through the night, and even then, if by some slim chance she does make it, her future could be a very cruel one." Numb with disbelief, David and Diana listened as the doctor described the devastating problems Danae would likely face if she survived. She would never walk, she would never talk, she would probably be blind, and she would certainly be prone to other catastrophic conditions from cerebral palsy to complete mental retardation, and on and on. "No! No!" was all Diana could say. She and David, with their 5-year-old son Dustin, had long dreamed of the day they would have a daughter to become a family of four. Now, within a matter of hours, that dream was slipping away.

Through the dark hours of morning as Danae held onto life by the thinnest thread, Diana slipped in and out of sleep, growing more and more determined that their tiny daughter would live, and live to be a healthy, happy young girl. But David, fully awake and listening to additional dire details of their daughter's chances of ever leaving the hospital alive, much less healthy, knew he must confront his wife with the inevitable. David walked in and said that we needed to talk about making funeral arrangements. Diana remembers, 'I felt so bad for him because he was doing everything, trying to include me in what was going on, but I just wouldn't listen, I couldn't listen. I said, "No, that is not going to happen, no way! I don't care what the doctors say; Danae is not going to die! One day she will be just fine, and she will be coming home with us!"'

As if willed to live by Diana's determination, Danae clung to life hour after hour, with the help of every medical machine and marvel her miniature body could endure. But as those first days passed, a new agony set in for David and Diana. Because Danae's under-developed nervous system was essentially raw, the lightest kiss or caress only intensified her discomfort, so they couldn't even cradle their tiny baby girl against their chests to offer the strength of their love. All they could do, as Danae struggled alone beneath the ultraviolet light in the tangle of tubes and wires, was to pray that God would stay close to their precious little girl. There was never a moment when Danae suddenly grew stronger.

But as the weeks went by, she did slowly gain an ounce of weight here and an ounce of strength there. At last, when Danae turned two months old, her parents were able to hold her in their arms for the very first time. And two months later-though doctors continued to gently but grimly warn that her chances of surviving, much less living any kind of normal life, were next to zero. Danae went home from the hospital, just as her mother had predicted.

Today, five years later, Danae is a petite but feisty young girl with glittering gray eyes and an unquenchable zest for life. She shows no signs whatsoever of any mental or physical impairment. Simply, she is everything a little girl can be and more.

Well...I wanted to show this to Elisa, but I knew that 90% of these stories on the internet were hoaxes. How could I check out this story?

Somewhere in the email was a reference to Irving, Texas. I lived in Dallas...and Irving was in our phone books as a suburb of Dallas. Is there a Blessing family in Irving? YES!!! There it was...A LOCAL CALL!!!

I called the number, and Diana Blessing answered. (Can you believe that???) I talked with her for a few minutes, explained our situation, and asked how Danae was doing. Danae was now 10 years old. Diana said that Danae was just doing great, and there were NO symptoms of the early birth. I then passed the phone to Elisa. I said, "Elisa…I think you need to talk to this lady."

Well that phone call was exactly what Elisa needed to boost her confidence in the future of CJ's health. And from then on, Elisa was considerably more relaxed with the situation.

Coincidence? Yeah…right. I don't think so. The folks up there know exactly what is going on, and they are there to help when we need them.

Elisa has been living with us all this time, and still is. She goes to hold her baby every day (40 minute drive), and CJ is up to almost 3 pounds now, and they have said CJ is now doing fine. We have grown very close to Elisa, and it has been a joy to be part of all this. AND…of course…this has brought our whole family, especially on my brother's side, VERY MUCH closer together. (Isn't that what Laurie said was going to happen?)

Baylor said that CJ could go home to Atlanta next week.

Interestingly enough, that Lisa had the baby here, where the facilities and doctors are the finest in the nation. But what is *more* interesting is when Patty said to me last week…I think we need to review the tape from the medium…I remember Laurie saying something about this.

Well…we had Shannon Maxey's reading all typed out on *Works*….from the tape we were given. Now, I take you back to October 3rd, 2001…and here is the tape. This is word for word…from the reading…

(There were a few lines here…I am eliminating them…)

Where's Lisa or Elisa?

Patty: Bob's niece.

Your daughter is acknowledging Lisa or Elisa. (Again)

(Several other lines here...then medium says...)

Bob.... your daughter is mentioning that you have a brother living?

Bob: I have a brother...Ronnie.

(Several other lines here...then back referring to Lisa...)

Is there any reason why your daughter would keep wanting to say hello to Elisa?

Bob: Not any more than anyone else. (I am baffled...and I have no idea.)

Well, go figure. Why would Laurie keep bringing up Elisa? Did she know something? Perhaps...as John Edward says, the folks up there really do know things, but they cannot tell us because we have "free will" to conduct our lives, and we will just have to wait for the future to unfold. But they sure can drop a few clues every now and then.

(Note from the future: as of October 2004, CJ is a fine, healthy, growing boy.)

Journal Entry: October 2, 2002

Laurie's birthday...Hi Dad!!

Background Info: Several months ago, I discovered a neat internet site that was called *Friends of John Edward*, hosted by Pam Blizzard. Pam also hosted a sister site called Spirit Discovery, which was for intellectual discussions relating to the spirit world. I used to go to the Friends site, but hardly ever posted on the Spirit site.

Now as I have mentioned, Laurie keeps sending me clues that she is watching. When I went to the medium Shannon Maxey on Oct 3, 2001, she told me that Laurie was always hanging around, and that Laurie will answer me when I call. Shannon also said Laurie was flying on my wing on all my Learjet flights.

I had not posted very much on Spirit Discovery...maybe a couple times. So I never got back much email from there. I saw a post in "Spirit Guides" dated July 28. On Sep 30th, I was answering a post 2 months old. Of course, I expected no one would answer for another 2 months. (What do I know.)

October 2nd...Laurie Ann's birthday.

As I was awakening this morning still somewhat in a meditative state I said, "Happy Birthday Laurie Ann....holler back, okay?"

After breakfast, I booted up the computer, checked email, and here was the first incoming...

Hello cbob, (Dated October 2)

loriann has just replied to a thread you have subscribed to entitled - *Everybody has them* - in the Spirit Guides forum of Spirit Discovery Forums.

Loriann?? So close...coincidence??

LoriAnn: Hello Everyone, I'm new to posting here....but for anyone who is trying this out, be patient and try to do it every night and it will happen!

<u>My return post:</u>

Cbob: Hi LoriAnn...Today, Oct 2, is my daughter's birthday...she died 20 years ago. Her name is Laurie Ann.

IrishRose: Here's to Laurie Ann - you are loved. Blessings, Irishrose.

Cbob: Thanks Rose....Just kinda weird to come out to the computer on Laurie Ann's birthday and see this in my inbox: "Hello cbob, loriann has just replied to a thread you have subscribed to..."

nozycat: cbob, my prayers to you and your wife. Nothing is just a coincidence, is it?

LoriAnn: Hello cbob, my prayers go out to you and your family. This was strange this morning that I posted at all. I usually just read. For some reason this morning I just felt a need to post something. Now I know why! Wow that is amazing how the spirits communicate with us. Blessings, Loriann

Cbob: HI again Loriann...I posted Laurie's story before on the other site. You can read it there if you want. She has contacted me before, using these "coincidences."

LoriAnn: Well, I have a feeling she was really nudging me. I have to tell you, I hardly ever post on boards. I am the type to sit back and learn. Now I know what made me! And today, the same feeling of "having" to post again! She must be a very strong and vibrant young lady to do this. You can post my message wherever you want. I don't mind at all. I have goosebumps all over! Blessings, Loriann

TxJude: Say "HI" to Laurie for me, will ya?

NOTE: The medium told me: Laurie is coming in so strong, that she must have had a very strong personality. Sounds just like what LoriAnn just said. And....that was her exactly....in this life.

(Thanks for letting Laurie use your site, Pam.)

BONUS from an Elf.

Well...here's the bonus. On that Spirit Discovery site, the thread I posted at was started by elfilosophy a few months previously. She did not give her real name. What do you suppose it was?

Elfilosophy (October 2, 2002) Location: Northwestern Ontario, Canada

Cbob...guess what? Just to add to the coincidence, I think I should tell you what my name is also. It's **Laurie Anne.**

I hardly ever posted there before...and without even knowing it...I posted on the one thread of Laurie Anne. Go figure.

Chapter 6

Contact, Mediumship and All That's Between

Journal Discussion: January 2003

Every year, we are getting to feel more and more "connected" to the other dimension, and it has developed good, positive feelings. As our connection grows, we both have become much less materialistic and more spiritual. I find myself having more sympathy for others and a much better perception of world events, which too often seem like "humanity insanity."

The connection has also brought Patty and I even closer together, as we now have a common "hobby" that we can share on a spiritual level, and we are both convinced that it is very real.

Yes...we can see and feel the changes. In addition, we have met many new friends and became closer to our relatives. My perception of life has improved.

Let's go on and see what 2003 will bring.

Journal Entry: Friday, Feb 21, 2003

John Edward Seminar...Dallas Convention Center.

Preliminary story.

A little over a year ago, John was in Dallas. Patty and I called in for tickets, but they were all sold out. We even called several times, and they were still sold out. I was not a happy camper, so on my next meditation I gave a piece of my mind to George, my Spirit Guide. I told him never do this to me again.

(I call my spirit guide George, for George Burns, because he is obviously a comedian. I figure that if he doesn't like that, he can tell me his real name.)

Well I never check John Edward's site, and figured that he wouldn't be in Dallas again for years. In the meantime, I converted another old Dallas friend of mine and his wife (Jack and Tanis) to *Crossing Over*. I told Jack all the things that happened to Patty and me and other friends and relatives, and how often coincidences just "happen to happen" at critical times. Jack and Tanis soon became solid fans.

Jack hardly ever went to JE's site either. However...one day in December Jack called me and was all excited. He said, "Hey Bob! I haven't been to JE's site for several months but out of the clear blue, I decided to go to JE's site this morning. Guess what? Brand new post...John is coming to Dallas on Feb 21, and the tickets just happened to go on sale today!"

Well...it took about 10 seconds to hang up and call the number...and we got 4 tickets.

Moral of the story: Don't underestimate your Spirit Guide...and be firm when you want something.

They were sold out within a few days, as usual. Luckily, my daughter Sheri and a friend of hers were able to get tickets also.

The seminar was scheduled for 6:30 pm, and doors open at 5:00 pm. Patty and I went to Jack's house, and we all went in their car. We arrived at 4:30 pm...two hours early. There was a light rain.

After parking, we went into the convention center, where there we encountered a line that appeared to extend into the state of Louisiana. Luckily, the line was inside the center, and extended down several hallways. (The center holds over 1700 people, and it was a full house.)

As we headed toward the end of the line, we came upon my daughter Sheri and her friend Vickie, so we stopped there for a chat. Soon, we were talking to the couple behind us, and boy was *that* interesting. It was a gal from San Antonio and her husband, who was a skeptic. She started telling some very amazing stories of spirits that have visited her and strange things that happened in their house. Several others in line got us all into a big circle, and we had like a little "party" going. (That was a stroke of luck, since by now everyone forgot that we crashed the line.)

But....here is the more interesting part...last September, this gal (and her hubby) flew to New York to see John, and she got a reading while in the audience and then a follow-up. She said it was absolutely mind-boggling, and that John had hit after hit about her family...everything was right on. So she now follows John around the country, this time in Dallas. Talk about an avid fan!!!! At least it helped the waiting time to go faster.

We got some pretty decent seats, about twenty rows from the stage, and we all sat together. At 6:35, someone came on and introduced John. Well, when John appeared...that whole place went bonkers!!! Everyone stood up and yelled their heads off...one section yelling, "we love you John" and the next section yelling "we love you more John" and on and on...GEEZ...for a minute I thought we were going to get into a fan riot about who loved John more.

After John tried for 5 minutes to quiet the place, they finally settled down, and John started into his "information discussion" and then took questions for awhile. About 7:00 pm, he began the readings.

I won't go into them much, except to say that he had about an 85% "hit" success, and...as normal...the other 15% consisted of folks who just had trouble remembering things. He was his unbelievable self...and very funny. The audience was in stitches so often that we weren't sure if we were at the Comedy Hour or John's seminar. Some of the folks were just like on TV...like John says, "Who is Abigail?" and the lady didn't know. Then John would say, "Yes you DO know because she is talking to me about you." Then...DUH...the lady would say "Oh, she was my sister-in-law who crossed." Same as on *Crossing Over*, right? John just never gives up, and he's right most of the time.

We did not get a reading, but we didn't expect one with 1700 folks there. But the seminar was not a disappointment. It was even worth much more than the $50 charge. Just to see him in person.

At the end when he asked for more questions, I tried to get one in, but he didn't pick me.

I was going to ask: "John...will we be getting out of here soon? We have to watch *Crossing Over* at 10:00 on Sci-Fi."

Journal Entry: Summer, 2003...Seeking more.

We learned of a "Development Circle" which was held on Wednesday nights each week in Plano by medium Kathleen Tucci, who was also an author. We decided to attend. She also had a couple of other mediums there who were just starting out in the field. It was a neat group, and good messages were passed around. Kathleen would also give readings for about an hour. The other mediums would occasionally provide some input.

On our first two attendances, I was hoping Laurie would make an appearance, but there was nothing for us either time. So on the day of the third session, I did some meditation in the afternoon, and I decided to enter some factors into the equation. I talked to Laurie's picture (of her and her horse, Jasmine) that was sitting on my desk, and I told her that I wanted her to mention my shoes, which I bought a half size too big. (But they were on a seventy-percent off sale, and Patty made fun of them.) Also maybe mention her horse.

As we drove to the place, I told Patty what I wanted to hear from Laurie...something about my shoes that I was wearing, or at least about her horse, or the name Jasmine.

About 30 minutes into the session, one of the amateur mediums was indicating a message coming in pulling her toward the area of the lady sitting next to us, and she asked the lady about a brown horse. The person did not know of any connection to a brown horse, and we did not answer. Then another medium said "there is also some connection to shoes here...like shoes that don't fit or something." The first medium interrupted and also said she was getting that too, from the same spirit. Patty and

I still remained silent, but we knew who it was for, and who it was from. Just another validation from Laurie.

The mediums often get messages, but are not sure who they are for. Often they know the area where the spirit might be pulling them, but not the specific individual.

Journal Entry: August 10, 2003

Did this bird have a ticket?

Patty's Story.

In June this year, my daughter called and said they were thinking about going on a cruise to celebrate their 15th anniversary. She was inquiring about prices, etc. and then asked if we would like to go along to help with the kids so they could enjoy themselves more. Bob immediately said 'sure'; so we begin making plans for a cruise. Bob got busy with a travel agent trying to get the best deals. I thought my mom who was 74 years old and had never been on a cruise might enjoy the experience so I sent her an email from work the next day and asked her if she would like to go with us.

Mom decided to go along on the cruise too. Bob got 3 rooms for the 7 of us and booked one of the grandkids in the room with my mom. We left here early in the morning one day before the day we were to set sail and headed for Houston to visit with Bob's daughter Lynda and her family. My daughter and her family, along with my mom, headed for Houston about mid afternoon after she and her husband got off work. We met at the motel there in Houston, and the next morning went to Galveston to board the ship.

On the second day of the cruise, we were well out to sea heading for Cozumel. Mom, my daughter and I were sitting on the deck by the pool talking and watching the kids swim. My mom mentioned how she thought my dad (crossed over) would have enjoyed something like this, and how she wished he could be here.

Within a few minutes of her saying that, a pretty little bird appeared from out of nowhere and flew over and landed on the back rail of the chair right next to where we were sitting. Keep in mind we are out at sea, a day and a half from port and there are no trees, no land...only water. We have never seen birds on a cruise ship this far out.

The bird sat on the back of the chair between us for about a minute just looking at us, and then flew off. In a few minutes it headed back over our way and flew right by a man sitting in the corner, but he never acknowledged the bird going by, he just sat there. Then the bird more or less just disappeared. My mother, my daughter and I all saw the bird, but from looking at the expressions of people around us, no one else appeared to have seen it. There is no doubt in any of our minds that the presence of the bird was my dad's way of letting us know he *was* with us. We never saw that bird or any other birds the rest of the trip.

Journal Discussion: January 12, 2004

What Dreams May Come.

During the course of my spiritual journey, I have learned that the spirit world uses dreams as an important and frequent means of communication. Larry has emphasized this many times in our discussions, and he has had many "visits" from his guide and other spirits through vivid or lucid dreams. On occasion, he has even been invited into astral travel and out-of-body experiences during his dream state. As recorded previously, Larry had a dream about the location of a lost airplane, and he led the sheriff right to it.

The reason that dreams can be "contact" experiences is that the brain has isolated itself from the entanglements of the real world and established a more relaxed condition. As a result, it can reach energy frequencies that the spirit world can tap into.

Therefore, over the past two years, I have read several books on dreams, and I have found this area a most fascinating study. By beginning the sleep cycle at night with meditation, I can fall asleep quite rapidly. But even more interesting is…that I can often "control" parts of the dream state. On occasion, my dream is very vivid and colorful, and I can remember more of the dream after awakening. In some dreams, I "feel" that I am a visitor in the spirit dimension, but I do not want to go too far with this. It is almost like an out-of-body experience, but not as realistic. Often I have played at length with my two loving pets that crossed many years ago...my dog Sydney and cat Bishi…and it seemed like I was really there with them in person.

In other vivid or lucid dreams, I have a "guide" (who I really don't know) and he takes me on tours around places….wherever we happen to be in the dream. Some of the places or events are pretty weird. Once I was on a long bus ride, but I had no idea where it was going. But I know I was interacting closely with many folks on the bus.

Some people and several books have said that dreams can sometimes "predict" events to come, or they can warn about an upcoming unpleasant experience. This could possibly be input from a spirit guide. Until this past year, I had not been into much of that. (But after giving it some thought…if they can nudge Patty in a conscious state to change lanes to avoid an accident, then the sleep state must be a cinch.)

However...I do recall a few dreams that did seem to foretell a coming event.

Looking back into April of 2002, I bought some ITWO stock at 3.79, thinking of course that it was near a bottom. I have never had dreams about the stock market before, but a few nights later, I had a very vivid dream that ITWO was at 1.56. I remembered it well after awakening. Well....I figured "no way" and anyway it was just a dream.

In June of 2002, I watched ITWO cross the wires at 1.56, and after I stopped kicking myself, I began to think twice about the dream. Was the dream a warning? Or was I stretching?

Back to Oct 6, 2003...Meditation Dream:

While meditating, I apparently fell asleep, and had this dream. I saw a man go up into my attic through the pull-down stairway and he was checking around the attic. I did not see who it was or his face. Then my Aunt Bunny who had crossed over about 40 years ago, told me he was checking to see if my attic was safe. (First dream I ever had of Aunt Bunny.)

I told her I didn't trust this guy, but she insisted he was ok. Later...I found the guy on a sofa with a blanket over him. When he removed the blanket, I saw that he had a very wrinkled face, like from a fire or something. I did not recognize him.

I asked him if there was anything that needed attention in the attic, and he said yes, you need to check your heating system. (Which is in the attic.) Then Aunt Bunny left, and the dream ended.

I went up there and checked around, changed the filter, and shrugged it off. It was working ok. This electric heater only serves the master bedroom...another gas heater serves the main house.

A few weeks later during the night we were fast asleep, and at 2:35 am the smoke alarm came on, and IT IS VERY LOUD. We both jumped up out of bed and there was a very strong smell of fire or smoke...a lot like strong car exhaust.

Patty said, "Oh MY GOD...THE HOUSE IS ON FIRE!" And I thought so too. We ran out of the bedroom, where the odor was not as strong. The house looked ok, but we did a thorough check everywhere, even outside. Nothing. But the strong odor was still in the bedroom.

We turned off the heating unit and opened the windows. After about 30 minutes, it began to clear up. We used the main house heater to permeate the bedroom. The next morning, I had my repairman come over to check it out.

He said the heating element failed, along with another problem causing the odor. He said "I could have caught this if you had done your yearly check-up last month."

I felt like saying, "Yeah...well...I'll certainly have you come back when the dead people tell me to."

As a skeptic, I now have thoughts in three areas about these events. One, that dreams are just dreams and just coincidences. Two, that some dreams may very well have "crystal ball" abilities but no one knows the source. And three, that some dreams do have input from the spirit world. Since my deceased Aunt Bunny was in one, and I hadn't given her a thought in ages, I am inclined to believe in the third case.

Journal Discussion: January 20, 2004... "The Nudge"

Nudge: to push gently; to draw the attention of; to give a hint to someone.

One of the ways the spirit world works is through a process that I call "the nudge." We all have free will on earth to make our own decisions. The sum of all those decisions in my past has put me here today in Dallas sitting at my computer after a fairly successful life and career…notwithstanding a few bumps along the way, of course.

But now…after learning that those decisions may well have had a "nudge" from the spirit world, I often reflect back in time, going back to think about all the decisions I made from high school to the present that have placed me where I am at this moment. Many of those decisions seemed pretty easy, and many were more confusing or complicated.

For instance, what event was it back in 1957 that made me decide to switch from Boston University to go to the Air Force Academy? That one decision made a dramatic impact on my path through life, especially as to location. I really had not intended to change course, but that event is a perfect example of the nudge:

Mom was very poor…no savings…no way to put me through college. I really wanted to be a pilot ever since I was a kid. So…I applied in 1956 for the Air Force Academy, and that education guaranteed you for pilot training upon graduation.

At that time you had to be sponsored by a US Congressman and take a week of tests at a near-by Air Force Base. I applied to all the Connecticut congressmen, and received a sponsorship from all four of them. Soon after, I went to Westover AFB for my tests.

The Academy was only in its second year then, so the classes were very small. There could be only 4 students from

Connecticut going into the class of 1960. I ended up as second alternate, number 6 and no one dropped out.

I applied for a scholarship to Boston University College of Aeronautical Engineering and received a first year full tuition scholarship, but it was dependent upon maintaining a very high scholastic grade that first year. However, I figured I would join ROTC and try to get to pilot training that way.

During the third semester, I was doing ok, and I had no intention whatsoever of going through that week of tests again for the Academy. I did not even apply.

One day, a letter came from one of the previous congressmen…Senator Prescott Bush (yes…George W. Bush's grandfather). The letter urged me to apply again, and he was going to automatically sponsor me. Well I just ignored that letter and threw it away.

A week later I received an urgent telegram from Senator Bush almost demanding that I go and take the tests again. Now…I don't even know this guy, and why is he so persistent that I try again??? (AHA!!! THE NUDGE)

Since he was so adamant, (like I felt I was in some kind of trouble if I didn't go) I decided to take the test and I was accepted. No more worrying about money, no more worrying about pilot training. I packed up and went to Denver (where the Academy first started out).

I now look back at those events and I am very certain that my spirit guide or someone up there was taking care of me, giving me that nudge, working through Senator Bush…the nudge that set the direction of my destiny and led into a successful and satisfying pilot career.

That may have been the most important nudge in my life, but there were certainly a lot more nudges, now that I look back and think about it. Larry told me about the "input" that he gets quite often from the folks. Not just in dreams, but in a conscious state, as they affect his decisions while flying or about his career or his spirituality.

Remember Patty's story about her moving to the other lane? Sure looks like a nudge from the folks to me. How about the "Beth" story from the medium…the nudge that got me to call Sheri and we found a new spiritual closeness. And Mister Bill certainly got a spiritual nudge from a few cell phone calls. Jack Weiss got a nudge out of the clear blue to visit John Edward's site and find Dallas tickets just going on sale. I am also sure the folks gave me a little nudge to read "*Hello From Heaven*" in the FBO, so Kathy could hook me up to Larry.

Then let's take the story of LoriAnn on my daughter's birthday when she said:

LoriAnn: Hello cbob, my prayers go out to you and your family. This was strange this morning that I posted at all. I usually just read. For some reason this morning I just felt a need to post something. Now I know why!

Quite often the nudge involves other people, as in some of the examples above. After being "connected" for a while, these events and coincidences begin to seem normal. Life becomes more and more connected every day. Everyone has the capacity to receive these nudges, but most people are just not tuned in.

BUT...IF YOU BUILD IT, THEY WILL COME.

Journal Entry: February 14, 2004

The Book.

When I was actively posting on Pam Blizzard's site, Friends of John Edward, I began to post some of my journal stories. The folks there kept asking for more, for which I felt quite honored. The stories became the center of good discussions. Soon, they made up a very large thread, and many of the folks told me I should write a book.

I had no idea how to get started on a book, so I just remained happy with expanding my journal. I figured if I were supposed to write a book, the "boys" would nudge me in some way so that it would just fall into my lap.

In the latter months of 2003, Patty and I were attending Kathleen Tucci's development circles every other Wednesday. At times, we would present one of our journal stories when it was appropriate to the subject being discussed. On one occasion, Kat asked us how many of these stories do we have? I answered, "About 45 pages in MS Works." She asked me to send her the entire journal. So I did on email.

Kat emailed back on January 13, 2004:

Bob! Your journal is absolutely awesome!!!!!!!! No kidding! I would really like to set up an appt when we can meet (preferably at my office) and discuss it in detail.

Well…I guess this means it fell in my lap. And we began discussions. And I had to quickly go through all my story files and put them in order and edit everything so as to be more in book format.

BUT WAIT!! THERE'S MORE!!

Early in the week of February 9th, Kathleen said she wanted to go meet Larry in Lebanon, and talk to him about his experiences for a few hours. I almost said, "I would Kat, but right now I am too busy writing a book."

I knew Larry was still flying, but he hardly ever comes to Dallas. So I was mentally preparing myself for the trip.

The "boys" went to work again, just like they always do. If they want you to do something, they create a path for you and make it easy. This is also their way of giving their approval, and providing that "nudge".

Larry calls us unexpectedly on Wednesday, February 11, and tells us that he has to fly down to Dallas-Fort Worth Airport and drop off some folks…then he can hang around and talk with us for a couple hours. (Ho hum, I am getting used to this by now, right?)

Larry landed at 3:30 pm and we all talked for about two hours and had a very informative discussion. And now Kathleen knows Larry personally.

Journal Entry: Saturday, February 21, 2004

During the week Larry called and said he would be here Saturday again, since he had to pick up the same folks he dropped off last week. This time, I picked up Larry at 11:30 am and we all had another great meeting with Larry, Patty, Kathleen, and her husband Lou for 3 hours.

Journal Entry: February 17, 2004

Background info: Patty and I have been playing "email scrabble" for about a month now while she is at work. I use the home computer, and we send our turns back and forth through the web site called "Bug Café". Bug Café decides what letters we each get. We take about 10 turns a day back and forth.

During meditation yesterday and upon awakening this morning, I talked to Laurie Ann and mentioned that I had not heard from her in a while, and I asked "how about a bit of contact soon, Laurie? Something out of the ordinary so I will recognize it easily."

When I went to the Bug Café site to get my letters and make a play, here are the letters I got:

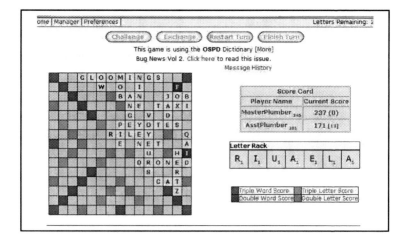

The letters unscramble to LAURIE A...and not a letter left over! What are the chances of that happening without help?

Journal Entry: March 4, 2004

Another message from Bill Sumrall.

After Bill's cell phone experience (just after his wife's mother crossed over), Bill began to "come around" that the folks *might* really exist in the afterlife, but he still had doubts. After all, it is pretty tough to convert an atheist. But at least he wasn't as adamant about his "there is no God" philosophy any more.

On January 5th, 2004 Bill's own mother crossed over. As he was about to leave to go to the funeral in Memphis, we talked a bit, and he asked if he will get a sign from his mother like Jan did. I told him that if he was open to it, it will occur and that I would throw it into my meditations.

Here is an email from Bill after returning to Texas.

Bill: Mom was buried in Memphis on Thursday, January 8th. On Friday morning...one day after we got back to Texas...I saw this white dove in the yard. In our 30 years here we have seen several types of doves but not one which is almost white. I called Jan to the window to see the dove and Jan immediately said it was a sign from mom. Eventually, three of these Ringed White Turtle-Doves seem to have taken up residence here.

My Audubon book says these types of doves were introduced and established in southern California, Arizona, Alabama, and southern Florida. (But rarely seen in Texas.)

Me: Bill...white doves are symbols of the spirit!! Jan is right...it *was* a sign from your mom!!

I went to a few internet sites involving doves, and sent these pieces to Bill:

The release of a white dove at memorial services symbolizes the spiritual message of hope and remembrance. A dove released at a graveside service brings closure for the family and all who attend. It is a special way to express a final "good-bye" and pay tribute to a loved one.

By releasing a single white dove at the graveside service, you are symbolically releasing their spirit. The single dove then joins the circling flock overhead, as if joining the angels before ascending to the heaven above.

White Doves represent spirituality in its deepest sense. Traditional funeral stories told that doves carried the souls of deceased people to heaven. Doves are often portrayed on graves to represent the eternal peace of someone who has departed this life.

Phone call to Bill: Well, Bill…are you convinced yet?

Bill: Well Bob, I am open. Jan said I was like the atheist guy in the town that was flooding rapidly. The guy is on the roof of his house as the water level rose toward the roof. He is shouting "Where are you, God…save me!!" And a rescue boat comes up to him. He says "Go away…I am waiting for **God** to save me." And then a helicopter drops down with a rope…and he says "Go away…I am waiting for **God** to save me." Then….as the water rises up to his neck, he shouts out "WHERE ARE YOU GOD…WHY DIDN'T YOU SAVE ME?" And then God's booming voice rang out from the clouds…. "Well…I sent you two rescuers, and you turned them down."

Yep…that's ole Bill. But I know he's coming around.

Journal Entry…Tuesday, May 18, 2004

They're foolin' with my scrabble game again.

As I mentioned before, Patty and I play email scrabble when she is at work. We also play bridge on Mondays,

Tuesdays, and Wednesdays (in the Microsoft Bridge Zone) from 6:00 – 8:00 pm on the computer with our internet friends.

Kathleen Tucci's standard announcement about another weekly development circle on Wednesday came in my email this morning. I sent Patty an email asking her if we should go to the meeting or play bridge Wednesday night. She emailed back and said, "I don't know yet. We have partners set up already on Wednesday. Let's play bridge unless the spirit guides tell us different."

Well…another email came in shortly after. It was my bridge pard saying that she had to cancel out for Wednesday. Of course, I could get another pard easily, but I decided to go to the gym for a workout first, then come home and figure it out.

I went to the gym in early afternoon and on the way home I decided to take a shower and then work on the journal a bit more. As I was driving home, I told my spirit guides that we haven't heard from them lately, and I sure would like to have some more journal entries, so get on the stick!! Also let me know if we should play bridge Wednesday night or go to the meeting. When I got back home, I checked the scrabble game on the computer to see if a turn was waiting for me from Bug Café. There was, and here are the letters that I had acquired!!! I about fell off the chair!!

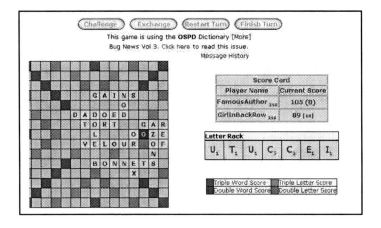

Clear as a bell...there was **TUCCI** sent to me in the new tiles!! I guess that was the folk's way of telling me to go to the meeting. Amazing! I told Kathleen at the meeting that I bet she never knew anyone whose spirit guide talks to them through a scrabble game.

Okay, now I am thinking... "Why was I *nudged* to go to the meeting?" Often, there is a nudge to do something, and the reason is not evident for a few days or weeks.

The meeting itself was quite interesting as a fellow named Stephen used psychometry to produce an astounding number of correct readings on two of the other folks attending. That in itself was quite amazing.

But there was something even more interesting that began to unfold. When I was selecting my clothes for the meeting, I decided to wear a shirt given to me by my NASA engineer kids, my daughter and her husband, Lynda and Jay. It was a sport shirt that had a space shuttle embroidered on the left upper side. It was the first time I have worn this shirt to the development classes.

At the meeting, a lady named Seema approached me and asked if I were some way connected to NASA. I told her that my daughter and son-in-law worked for NASA. She said she had a brother named Andy who strongly needed guidance in his upcoming career. He was an engineering student at Stanford and he wanted to work for NASA but he did not know how to go about it. I told her to have Andy email me, and I would pass it on to Lynda and Jay.

The next day, I emailed Seema and asked if she also had a "nudge" to go to that meeting. This was her reply:

May 28, 2004
Hi Bob:

Yes, I absolutely did feel that nudge to go to last Wednesday's meeting. I got lucky and was able to go because my mother happened to be visiting. (I have a 2 month old who needed to be babysat and my husband had plans). Then as I was about to leave, my brother called and clearly needed guidance about his career that I could not provide. I told him that I was going to my psychic group and that I had a feeling I would get something while I was there. Before the group started, I saw you and your wife come in and I just had the urge to talk to you. Then you sat down and I saw your shirt with a rocket logo and I thought "that's weird." But then I knew you were a pilot so you probably couldn't help me with Andy's dilemma. And then you mentioned your daughter working as an Aero Engineer with NASA and I thought, "That's it!"

I was so excited that Andy's guides pulled through for him. Andy emailed me his list of questions for your daughter. I'm going to put these in a separate email.

Thanks! Seema

May 29 Andy writes to Lynda and Jay:

Dear Lynda and Jay,

My name is Andy Sadhwani and I am a graduate student in Mechanical Engineering at Stanford University. I am very grateful for this opportunity to email you as I understand that Lynda is working as an Aeronautical Engineer at NASA. I have been interested in Rocketry as long as I can remember and my dream job would be to help design and build rockets. Over the winter holidays, I taught Rocket Science as a merit badge during Boy Scout Camp. I also recently won 1st place in a Model Rocket Design competition at Stanford.

June 5...Jay writes back and answers Andy's questions in a very long email, and they set up a tour for Andy when he comes to Houston on June 10.

June 10...Jay and Lynda give Andy a personal tour of NASA, and much guidance for his career. Andy emails us all that afternoon.

Dear Bob, Jay and Lynda,

Thank you all very much for setting up a NASA tour for me. It was really exciting meeting the engineers and seeing the technology. In addition it gave me wonderful insight into how NASA operates. As I've told my sister, this behind the scene look into NASA is exactly what I needed. I am going to submit my NASA application within the next day or two.

Andy S.

June 10...Afternoon...Email from Seema

Bob:

As you probably know by now, Andy met Jay and Lynda and had a great tour at NASA. He is very grateful to you for getting the ball rolling for him. If you hadn't followed your gut and come to Kat's group, none of this would have happened. Andy is a talented young man who is able to think outside of the box and is also a hard-worker. He has expressed to me that his only true desire in life is to help humanity through space exploration. You have opened new doors for him and in his own words, given him a major stepping stone in his life.

Seema

This is a perfect example of how spirit guides work. Just as the nudge from Prescott Bush was involved in the launch of my own career back in 1957, I now have experienced the nudge on the other side of the equation. I was nudged to go to that meeting because someone else needed help. I am beginning to think that the spirit guides are all in collusion up there and they plot very intricate ways to guide us here on Earth.

<u>Journal Entry: Tuesday, May 25, 2004</u>

"Smile…You're on Candid Camera."

     Background Info: Back in May of 2001, Patty and her two sisters decided to get together with their mother for a Mother's Day celebration and family reunion. She took our good camera, which had higher ASA speed film in it. That way, she didn't have to use the flash. They had the celebration at Kathy's house, Patty's younger sister. Kathy had recently lost her husband Bobby due to a heart attack. They took a lot of pictures.

     After developing the photos, we noticed that one of them, in the upper right corner, had a blue streak with a white orb showing. It did not look like a reflection or a camera fault, but we just assumed that it was. Patty put the streaked picture and a few of the others in the framework of the hutch to make a kind of photo gallery. Sometimes I would look at it and wonder just what could have caused that streak. We never had the camera do that before, and all the other photos were normal. Kathy is on the right near the blue streak. It is her house. On the upper left is Carolyn and in the center is Patty. Below is Nana.

In one of our development circles with Kathleen Tucci a few months ago, we had a discussion of spirit images being caught on film, and some of the descriptions fit perfectly the image of our photo. Still, I did no further investigation into the phenomenon, even though the picture was in plain view every day.

Present day: I am reflecting back now to the development circle last Wednesday, when the "scrabble game" told us to go to that meeting. I decided to take the photo to the meeting for Kathleen's interpretation. Kathleen didn't even hesitate...she explained the entire streak and identified it as a typical spirit image.

Well...now my skeptic side begins to appear. How do we *really* know it is not just a reflection? So this morning I went into Google and searched "spirit pictures" and found a lot of sites with a lot of pictures and a lot of explanations.

Lo and behold...dozens of the same kind of blue-streaked pictures were on these sites, verified as spirit images (or at least verified as <u>not</u> reflections). The streak looked exactly like in our photos. Here are two from the site: http://www.crystalinks.com/amanda.html.

We now believe that it was Bobby's energy captured in the photo...he came to visit Kathy just like spirits do at family gatherings. You just can't beat this belief in the spirit world...the folks not only play around with you, they let you take their pictures. Life is good.

Journal Entry Continued: Katherine Baker's story

After writing the previous entry, I remembered that Kathy had mentioned a "spiritual experience" when Bobby died. Patty wrote to Kathy and asked her to send her story on email.

Katherine Baker's Story:

I have been asked to retell the story of what went on with my guardian angel and me February 27, 2001, the day my husband Bobby died.   This was a crisp February morning, nothing out of the ordinary, until I started to work. I live in a very small East Texas town and I drove daily to a job 40 miles away in Greenville, Texas.

This morning as I was leaving for work, I kissed my husband goodbye, as usual, and told him I loved him. He was handicapped, and was home each day alone due to blindness.

That day, as I was entering the small town of Lone Oak, I heard a noise like someone had hit the side my car with their fist. I pulled over to the shoulder of the road and looked at the car, the tires, etc. trying to figure out if I had ran over something or what had caused the noise.

Well, I found nothing, so I got back in my car and drove less than a mile when I went around a sharp curve in the road, and traffic was stopped dead still in front of me. There was a long line of cars up the road a little ways on a bridge. I saw fire trucks and ambulances and police cars everywhere. I thought "Oh no, a wreck and I am going to be late to work," but immediately I thought about what had just happened back down the road less than a mile. Something had caused me to stop my car and get out and look at it. Little did I know at the time that it was probably my angel trying to stall me so I would not have been on that bridge at the time of the accident. If I had not stopped, the timing would have probably been perfect for me to have been the one in the head-on collision.

As I sat in the traffic waiting for them to clear the road, I thought I would call home and ask Bobby if there was another route I could take (he knew all the back roads). So I called him on my cell phone but when it rang, it sounded like someone just picked the phone up and dropped it. I hung up thinking my battery must be low, so I plugged it in to recharge. After about 10 minutes of waiting, I tried to call my house again. This time a policeman answered my phone "Fletcher Residence" and I immediately panicked. I asked who he was and why he was answering my phone. The nice man on the other end asked who I was and asked if I was Bobby's wife and when I told him who I was, he told me to turn my car around and get home as soon as I safely could. I asked what was wrong and he would not tell me. So I made a few phone calls to my sister-in-law and my daughter who both lived close by. Neither of them were at home, so I kept trying until I found someone and I was told that my husband had just had a massive heart attack and died. Needless, to say I was in shock.

I turned my car around to start back home but I stopped to have a cry when my pastor called and told me to just stay put because he and his wife would be coming to get me and drive my car home. I was sitting in the car on what I thought was the shoulder of the road with my head down on the steering wheel crying my eyes out when all of a sudden I heard something and looked up. There was the nicest, cleanest, neat looking middle age man getting out of a van and walking back to my car. I don't know where this van could have come from, because both lanes of traffic were stopped so no one could have gotten through.

He walked up to my car and said, "Ma'am, I am here to help you. I know you are in distress; I don't know what your problem is but I was sent here to help you."

I started crying and told him that I had just gotten the news that my husband was dead. He helped me get my car off the road and to safety at a nearby roadside park. This man offered me something to drink and brought me Kleenex and told me he would stay with me until my preacher could get there. I have never seen this man before and only saw him once since. I kept asking him his name and he told me I didn't need to know his name; he was just sent to help me and his name wasn't important. He stayed with me consoling me until my pastor got there and he left.

Minutes later as we went through the town where I had stopped previously because of the noise I heard in my car, this young man was standing on the side of the road hitchhiking.

Now, I know God sent this man to me in my time of need. I don't know what happened to the van he was driving earlier. I believe without a doubt that he was my guardian angel that day from the time I heard the noise and stopped my car, which could have helped me avoid the head-on collision, to being with me during the saddest day of my life.

Yes, there definitely are guardian angels.

Journal Entry: Sunday, August 15, 2004

They're still hangin' around.

Every so often the folks will let us know that they are still hanging around. They do that in very interesting ways. I have become accustomed to their little tricks...usually through electrical interferences. These folks are very innovative. And their activities have become so common that I don't even write a lot of them in the journal.

However, sometimes they will be silent for weeks, and I will get no signs of their presence. I usually meditate three or four times a week and try to communicate with them in that fashion. But when I don't hear from them for a while, I start getting really firm in the meditations....asking them to "do something funny."

On Thursday, August 12, I suffered a setback on an investment, and I began doing everything I could to keep the negative energy from dominating my brain. I had not heard from the folks in weeks. On Friday morning, I decided to meditate, and I was quite firm with them, "Okay guys!! I really need some signs here...and NOW would be a good time!"

These events happened on Friday, August 13:

After meditation, I went to the computer to see if there was any new email. At 10:50 am, as I was reading one email...not even touching the keyboard or mouse...the screen went totally blank and the power unit started making noises. I was about to panic, as my first thought was that the puter just crashed. But after a few seconds...the screen began to flicker with the beginnings of a boot-up. Then the desktop re-appeared. What a relief!

But I was baffled...the computer did a warm boot *all by itself*...I had not touched it. I never saw a computer do that before. But everything was normal, so I just brushed it off as a "Twilight Zone" event.

(Now here is a little background information. I have a cordless combination phone/answering machine on the hutch, about 10 feet from my meditation chair. I had shut off the answering feature about two years ago, and it has never made a peep since then.)

After reading the email I went into my chair and continued reading my latest book *Mind Science*. After reading about ten pages, my thoughts were interrupted by a woman's voice saying quite loudly out of nowhere... **"PRESS THE U KEY TO RECEIVE FURTHER INSTRUCTIONS."** That was it. At first, I had no idea where it came from...seemed just like a weird "Twilight Zone" occurrence. Then I realized that it could only have come from the telephone speaker, which had been silent for two years. DUH!!! The folks are pulling their tricks again!! I could not figure out the significance of the message itself, but it certainly caught my attention. (I checked to see if there was an incoming call, but there were no incoming phone calls that morning. Besides, the answering machine was still in the OFF position.)

About two hours later, I was at the computer again. As before, I was not touching the keyboard or mouse, and the old "warm boot trick" was repeated. I said out loud, "HEY GUYS...quit messing with my computer!! Mess with some other stuff!!"

The rest of the afternoon was normal.

But wait! There's more!

Patty came home from work and we had dinner. After dinner, Patty went to the bedroom and turned on the TV. She came out of the bedroom and said "The satellite must be broken...there is no TV."

Sure enough, the only thing on the screen was "Insert a valid access card." Well this card had been valid for two years, and it was not supposed to expire. So I called Direct TV and asked them why I got this message. The woman on the other end said, "We have no idea...your card is still valid according to our records. Try this...take the card out and unplug the TV...then reinsert the card and turn the TV back on." I did that, and it worked. I asked her why it did that, and she said she did not have a clue. (Well...I knew why it did it...I was just checking to see if SHE knew.)

It was the first time I ever had to re-boot the TV. That was the FOURTH electrically related incident of the day. I said, "OK GUYS...THANKS...YOU CAN GO TO BED NOW."

I know they laugh at me. But that's okay...it's my own little world.

What I have accomplished...

As I wrap up my journal for now, I do so without really having "developed" my psychic powers to any great degree. I am still working on that. I have certainly become more "sensitive" in many psychic areas, and certainly more open and receptive to the spirit world and my own consciousness. But as John Edward says...

"You don't need to be a medium to work with the Other Side; you just need to be open to the vibrations and be willing to listen."

Anyone can achieve this closeness to spirit. You just need to put in a little effort, learn to meditate, and truly believe it can be done.

While our spiritual journey is far from over, at this point I can reflect upon what improvements it has made in our lives since we began in September of 2000.

Our spiritual journey:

1. Has given us a belief system that makes complete sense, can be verified, and fills in the "gaps" that I have always felt from the strict, established religions and doctrines. In addition, it has given us a stronger awareness that a "God" does exist.

2. Has changed the way we perceive this life on earth as humans, since materialistic values become less important and are slowly being replaced by spiritual values. Events happening here are more understandable now, and they are easier to deal with when seen in relation to the other side and the spiritual parameters.

3. Has completely removed our fear of death (as most NDE's will tell you, you get to see the ceiling for a while, then move on through the tunnel to HOME).

4. Has programmed our spiritual self to be more in tune with our physical being. (This is hard to explain unless you are well into your journey.)

5. Has given us much comfort in knowing that my daughter, relatives, and friends who crossed over are not dead, but watching us and waiting for us in the afterlife. I can finally "let go" of the guilt and sorrow...knowing I will see them again. And even to "feel" their presence here on earth.

6. Has brought us a host of new friends, in person and on the internet, many who already were ahead of us (like Larry), and some who became convinced after we presented our case. And sharing all this with them is a blessing in itself.

7. Has brought our families much closer together...particularly on my brother's side and with my own wife and daughters.

8. Has taught me how to meditate...and talk to the folks...and wait patiently for them to answer...and they always do. (Not to mention the health benefits.)

We are looking forward to more in the future...because it just gets better.

Note: While the book portion of my journal ends here, I continue my spiritual journey through our web site:

www.connectingtospirit.com

Here you will find other interesting spiritually related web sites, stimulating articles, and much of the spiritual information that helped me in the learning process.

Journal Appendix 1

Bob's comments

My first "retirement" from aviation was in 1996, when the company I worked for was bought out and I was sort of "forced" to retire. By 1999, I was really missing the flying, and I was thinking about getting recurrent again, which would cost about $7000. Even then, I would have to go looking for a job, and at my age, that was pretty "chancy". I was not into the spirit world then, but during that summer, I really started praying for "one more chance" to continue my pilot career for a few more years. Apparently, my spirit guide (which I really wasn't aware existed at the time) still heard me, because...just as it has happened many times before in my life...the "nudge" came along. This time it was through an old pilot friend, Buron Robison. Buron and I were pilots together with the old company. Although Buron was still flying, he was also looking for a new company to work for. I had not seen or heard from him in 4 years.

In early 1999, Buron landed a good job as a chief pilot with a company called AmeriPlan in Dallas, and for now he was the only pilot. For many months he had been using "contract" pilots for the co-pilot position, since the jet requires two people.

Buron continues here...

After several months of using contract pilots, I was told by the bosses to find a permanent pilot to work with me. I was looking around, but kept running into snags all the time. One applicant had too little flying hours to be accepted by the insurance company. Another could not pass the physical. Several applicants were way too large to fit into our small Lear cockpit. Some of them I knew I would not get along with on a permanent basis.

One day I hired a contract pilot named Bob. As I was getting into the cockpit that day, the name "Bob" just somehow translated into Bob Dean. I had no idea how that name just "popped" into my head, because I had not heard from him in many years.

I immediately went to the office and called Bob...he had the same phone number as he did way back in the old days. He said something like, "What took you so long?" He had been retired for some time, which I didn't know, but I quickly got him up to speed on the Lear.

And we had a good two and a half years of great flying together. Near the end of 2000, I watched Bob get into the spiritual thing, and during the next year he started telling me his and Patty's stories. I was already receptive, since I had a few things happen in the past that were similarly related. It was very interesting to see him grow in that area, and especially when he found Larry and we all went to Larry's house. I still see Larry sometimes on our Lebanon layovers.

P.S. He saved the company money too, getting those spirits to fix that cell phone (grin).

Buron Robison
Chief Pilot, AmeriPlan

Bob Comment: The pilot job was a real plus in my spiritual journey, for many reasons. But mainly...I would have never met Larry if it did not come along. One can say that all this was just coincidental, but in truth I know that the folks up there were taking care of me, just as Larry says they do.

It is all connected.

Journal Appendix 2

Larry's Comments

I try to be a private person about my knowledge of and belief in the spiritual dimension, because many people and religions are just not into this. I even got myself into some trouble with my church when I tried to explain my near death experience to them. They were not very understanding. So I just left that church and found a more understanding one.

However, my experience over 20 years ago profoundly changed my life and the way I perceive the universe and God and our temporary existence here on earth. It really doesn't matter to me what any religion preaches, because I KNOW what is the real story, and there is not an iota of doubt in my mind. The connection to my spirit guides is an awesome experience, and it gives me great comfort while I finish up here on earth.

As to my near death experience, skeptics can say "you were dreaming" and things like that, but how can they explain my gift of automatic writing? Or the psychic inputs that I experience in my dreams? Or how I can find a lost airplane that crashed? Or the "coincidences" that I experience on a regular basis that help me conduct a better life and keep me out of trouble? Or the out-of-body experiences and astral travel?

When Bob Dean called me on Sunday, July 15th, 2001…of course I was a bit cautious about talking to a stranger. But once I became comfortable about his spiritual journey, I could open up, and believe me…I like to talk about it. Now we discuss it regularly.

He asked me if I ever watched John Edward or read about other mediums, and I just said, "Who's John Edward?" All of my knowledge came from my spirit guides, and it appears to be totally in tune with what John Edward says and what Bob has learned. When I "died"…and through automatic writing…I learned from the guides such things as why we exist…how and why we should be spiritual...much guidance as to how to proceed in my life...and much about the metaphysical universe. There was so much knowledge and information introduced to me that I could never possibly cover it all. But our purpose in this life is to love our fellow man and God, pursue a spiritual course, and help others as best we can. If everyone believed this way, there would be no more wars, or crime, or murders.

For all those who choose to pursue this course into spiritualism, I guarantee that your life will be enhanced...and it will take on a new, more beautiful meaning. And it just gets better all the time.

Larry Hastings

Journal Appendix 3

Sheri's Story... Part 1

I was 14 in August of 1980. Mom, Lynda, Frank (mom's husband) and I had recently moved from my childhood hometown of Irving to some unknown little East Texas town called Palestine. I was separated from my school friends, and knew no one in Palestine. I was not a happy camper. Laurie was 16 and had a car, and chose to live with dad in Dallas and stay in the Irving school.

The phone rang in the very early morning of August 16, 1980. That call changed my life dramatically, and in many ways is still having an effect on my life. My oldest sister Laurie had an accident and was in the hospital. No details were given. We all made a fast trip to Dallas at 4 am. It seemed like mom knew the end result, but was trying to stay unemotional.

At 6:30AM our family of four rushed into the emergency room. Nurses scattered. Finally, someone told us to wait in an office that was down a darkened hall. The doctor will be with you soon, they said.

When the doctor came in, he told us my sister had died. I remember thinking that he made a mistake...it couldn't be! I was stunned. Later that day, family members began to gather in Dallas from out of state. My grandmother stayed with us at my dad's house after she arrived.

The next day I was emotionally spent, physically exhausted, and very angry at God for doing this. The whole situation still seemed surreal, but the pain was very real. My grandmother was drinking a cup of coffee at the breakfast table, and was trying to give me comforting words. "God has a plan, everything will be all right, don't be angry..." and other things that a fairly religious person would say to a kid trying to cope with the first death in the family. Whatever, grandma! All I felt was that if this is God's plan, then me and this God guy aren't going to get along very well.

How could God do this to a 14 year old kid? The memories I have over twenty years later are still very vivid and horrible. Shopping for a casket, attending the wake, what will Laurie wear, the burial. God...please don't do me any favors. I think your plans suck! After the funeral, we tried to resume life in Palestine.

A few weeks later, I was asleep and had a very vivid dream. It was Laurie, and she came to see me. This dream was very different from any dream I ever had...like it was very real. Although the visit was brief, a lot of information was exchanged. The dream went like this:

> I was sitting on the floor in my bedroom Indian style, looking up at Laurie, who was sitting on my bed. The feeling I had was calm and matter-of-fact, and I was not at all scared. Very calmly I asked her: "So...what's it like there?" In a nonchalant manner and nodding her head left and right, she said it was okay, and we began a conversation.

When I awoke, I knew that things had just changed for me because of that "visit". I knew now that there was an afterlife, and I was no longer afraid of death. I had a deeper understanding of life in general, although I couldn't say exactly what that new understanding was. I had always felt a creepy nervousness about death, but after Laurie's visit, even though I was still angry about her having died, I myself no longer feared death. Laurie gave me some kind of peace that I had not had before, and that helped me cope tremendously.

Part 2

Shortly afterward, I had my first out-of-body experience, although I did not know at the time what it was. I was lying on my bed ready to go to sleep. I was either asleep or beginning to fall asleep when I felt a sudden "lightness" about me. Then, very quickly, I was lifted up a ways and over to the corner of the room looking at my body sleeping in my bed! It seemed very real...not like a dream. I will never forget the feeling I had at the time.

Part 3

When my sister Lynda was pregnant with her first child, mom and I went to her house in Houston in December. Lynda wanted a girl.

Our sleeping arrangements put me in the room that would be the baby's room. During my sleep, I saw the face of a young child. Nothing was said to me, I just saw a face.

When I woke up, I went to Lynda and started telling her things like, "You are going to have a boy with dark brown eyes. He will be born about two weeks early on an even numbered day. He will be average weight, but longer than average." In all, there were about ten things I rattled off, and the weird thing is, I do not know how I got this information. I don't remember any conversation in the dream, only the child's face. Lynda wrote all the premonitions down.

As it turned out, Justin was born about two weeks early on February 22, and most all of the other things I said were true.

Then one day when Justin was about 18 months old, Lynda, Jay, and Justin were at our house. Justin was walking in the living room, and turned around and looked in my direction. Then it hit me. I looked at Lynda and said "Remember when I told you I saw a child's face before Justin was born? Well...THAT IS EXACTLY THE FACE I SAW!" Even details such as his hair were the same as what I saw that night.

Part 4...August 2001

In July of 2001, I began to realize that I had been through many weird experiences that I could not explain and I did not fully understand. I was not sure about what was behind a lot of things that happened to me. Why did I separate from my body? How did I know about Justin? How did Laurie communicate with me? Was I psychic? Do other people experience this?

In August, my husband Jody and I were watching a show on television that had a guest named George Anderson. He was a psychic medium...someone who "speaks to the dead." But what he was saying on that show began to make sense to me within the framework of my experiences, so I immediately went out and bought his book. After reading the book, all of a sudden I began to make sense of everything. It was coming together! It was opening up a whole new world for me.

Then...as a big added bonus...my dad calls me in October and tells me he thinks Laurie is capable of communicating with us. That's where I said "Sit down Dad...this telephone conversation is going to last a few hours."

(Like...Hey Dad...been there...done that.)

A Note from Kathleen

After reading Bob's journal, you probably have many more questions than you had when you started.

In the next few chapters, I will elaborate on some of the psychic and spiritual experiences of Bob and Patty as their journey began to unfold. I will cover Spirit Guides, dreams, developing psychic reception areas, and physical death, including a more detailed story on Larry Hastings.

Chapter 7 Get to Know
Spirit Guides and
Master Teachers

Many are under the impression that we must surrender control of our consciousness to allow our guides to speak through us in a form of channeling, or that by creating a relationship with your Spirit Guide you are no longer in control of your own destiny. This is not true. Everyone has one or more Spirit Guides, and you need not possess mediumistic abilities to communicate with them. You do not need to give up your conscious control, for they will speak to you with a thought that drifts through your mind like a feather in the wind. They will lead you with an inner prompting along the path that you agreed to travel and they will also act as a go-between in spiritual activities. They are your best friends if you will accept their assistance and strive to trust them.

Many of us believe that we have only one Spirit Guide. This is also a misconception. We do have one Spirit Guide that remains with us for all of our lives who is referred to as our Master Teacher or Master Guide, but we have many others as well. Let's take a look at them.

Master Guide

Master Guides are usually self-realized, very spiritually advanced beings. They have always inhabited a spiritual body. Master teachers oversee the growth and development of many people. They do not limit themselves to just one individual. Our relationship with our Master Guide is something that manifested in the ethereal plane before coming to earth. In other words, we and our Master Guide collectively decided that we would work together while in this particular incarnation on earth. Their job is to keep you on-track with your individual soul's purpose. Your job is to use their expertise and assistance to your greatest advantage in elevating your soul to a higher consciousness both here on this plane and in the spiritual plane later.

Spirit Guide

The general characteristic that separates a Spirit Guide from other types of spiritual beings is that most have lived a physical life. Their purpose is to aid others in working through the same lessons that they have been through. The Spirit Guide is here to help with problem solving. They can often appear in groups as well as a single entity. It's important to know that these Guides are learning just as we are, and although their perspective is much broader than ours, they often remain in the background watching to see how we solve our problems. They provide insight through dreams or meditation, or they might implant the "sudden realization" of a developing situation and our role in that situation (the proverbial "light bulb going off"). They usually stay only for a set amount of time based on our growth and our need for their expertise. As some Guides leave because they are no longer needed in certain areas of our life, other Guides will enter to aid us in new ways of development and learning. Some Guides can also be relatives that have since passed in this lifetime but have a keen interest in our well being. Imagine a college setting...you have one teacher for Math, one for English, one for Biology etc. So it is with your Spirit Guides. They assist us in matters of health, science, relationship skills, and other areas. The Master Teacher is, in comparison, the Dean of the school, overseeing the curriculum of all the other Guides. The Spirit Guides are here to help us develop principles regarding our morals, compassion, and ethics. They work hand in hand with our Master Guide.

How Do We Get To Know Our Guides?

Guides contact us in very subtle ways. They provoke a thought in our head, they visit us in our dreams and appear in our meditations. Like all concepts in spiritual growth, your intent is everything and if you desire to make contact with guidance, your dedication and perseverance will enable you to do so. Some Guides appear as physical beings in meditation and dreams while at other times they appear as beings of light. You can ask your Guide to appear in your dreams, but better still is requesting your Guide to meet with you while in meditation. Like all spiritual beings, Guides seldom predict the future. While they give you some hints as to what may occur if you continue on your current path, it is not their responsibility to tell us what to do. In life threatening situations they will attempt to warn us but they will not give us the lottery numbers.

Your Spirit Guides will make themselves known in a variety of ways. Some will use symbols, or synchronous events that we assume are coincidences, that lead us down a certain path. Others may help you to experience a feeling of warmth or coldness, or a touch on a particular part of your body each time they are near. Others may be more auditory. This can range from a simple buzzing or ringing in your ears to actually hearing whispers or voices if you're persistent and diligent with meditation. Some Guides will present themselves through colors or fragrances. Others may simply show themselves as they once were in the physical. Spirit Guides are also distinctly male or female.

Most will give names, but some will not. Names are not as important as the information that comes through. Ask your Guides for names anyway, as it helps to personalize the relationship you have with them. Trust the first name you get, even if it doesn't seem to fit. I say that because many guides will give you a name that you can remember and relate to. It is not unusual for the name given to be a common household name. Guides, in whatever manner they emerge, use an appearance that will be comfortable for you.

Attitude is crucial for connecting with our Spirit Guide in a balanced, grounded manner. If you are serious and approach it with a common sense attitude, you will eventually succeed. Please note the need for patience. Fear and impatience are the largest stumbling blocks that hinder or distort the connection. Know that Guides will never try to trick you even in teaching, and they will only be there to support you and aid in your education as a soul. Speaking with Guides takes a lot of practice, but the reward is tremendous.

A Spirit Guide will always offer encouragement and build you up. He or she will display great love and respect for you. If the message you receive from a Guide is even faintly disparaging, then it is not a message from a true Spirit Guide. It is either a product of your own mind or that of the Medium. Or, it could be a genuine message from a Spirit who is not a guide, but one who is not worth talking to. Spirit Guides always display the utmost love, wisdom and discretion. They encourage you to live your own life the best way you can and they will guide your journey, but never direct it. That is where your personal responsibility comes in.

There is a misconception about the psychic and metaphysical world and the path to higher spirituality. Many assume that if they are not working actively in the psychic field or they don't know who their Guides are, they are not making progress. They feel that if they are not demonstrating psychic ability, they are not growing. But It is not the demonstration of psychic ability or a personal conscious communication with Guides that unfolds our potential. Our potential and the reflection of it can be seen in the meeting of our daily trials and obligations in a creative manner that propels us along our individual paths. The purpose of contact with the spirit realm is that we nurture the ability to look beyond physical limitations so that we can see ourselves as spiritual beings of light with endless possibilities.

This is a letter from one of my clients regarding Spirit Guides that I thought was interesting.

Dear Kathleen:

I wanted to let you know that I heard you on the radio this morning. You did a good job! I took my oldest daughter to school this morning and she happened to turn it to one of her favorite radio stations...and there you were. I also wanted to share with you something that I found interesting that I ran across. One of the children I was testing for Aspergers had experienced seeing "someone" (who no one else could see) standing outside of his car. He had an anxiety attack over it. The psychologist that I was working with was afraid that this boy might have a form of schizophrenia. I was afraid that this would become an issue. Since I have developed my spirituality and have learned what I know now, I was afraid that the psychologist would diagnose him wrong. But, as it turned out this psychologist spoke to the student about these events. The student explained that he only sees this person when he is afraid or sad. The student also said that he is no longer afraid of this person he saw. And...to top it off, guess what...the person that he keeps seeing is an Indian! When the psychologist told me this I just laughed and commented... "Why are they always Indians?" He grinned with me. The psychologist just told me that since this Indian person was not telling the student to do anything bad and it seemed to help him, that he did not think that he had a form of schizophrenia. I was relieved that the psychologist did not put the wrong diagnosis on this student. Of course my Guide is not an Indian. I guess I have to be DIFFERENT!

Have a great weekend,
Melinda

Here is another story which I feel shows a clear example of what can happen when you follow those "hunches" your Spirit Guide gives you.

Sent from Jane:

While I was in Texas visiting, I expressed interest in going to Tioga, Texas to find the cemetery where my great grandparents are buried. I had a strong urge to see it for some reason and didn't want to leave Texas without doing so. Reba (a friend's mother), her husband, my parents and I all took the ride over to Tioga. We traveled for about an hour I think until we came to the town. We had to stop and ask a local store clerk if he knew where the old cemetery was. He sent us up a sparsely traveled road and soon we were there. We got out and were walking around the site looking for my ancestors. I found them! There they were next to each other with some other family members as well. The others were walking around up on a hill when I called out to them to let them know. I was kneeling on the ground planting flowers on my great grandparent's graves (who I never knew) and this cowboy in a pickup truck comes pulling up. He got out and as he started over to me he looked startled and stopped in his tracks. I was thinking, "What's wrong, am I in some sort of trouble? Who is this cowboy?" I said hello to him and asked him if everything was okay. He said, "Are you putting flowers on those graves?" I said, "Why yes. These are my great grandparents." He then said, "Well they are my great grandparents too!" The others were starting down the hill toward us and they wondered what was wrong. My mother came to us and asked if everything was okay. The man stopped again, big tears spilled from his eyes and he said, "You look exactly like my mother! (His mom was deceased and he had come on his yearly visit to see her gravesite.) He said he had been thinking of going to the little cemetery for some time and just that day and that hour had decided to drive down at the very same time we went! We stayed for about an hour and my mother knew some of his grandmother's (my grandmother's sister) people. No one else showed up at the cemetery and he said no one is ever there much since it is pretty old and out of the way. We exchanged phone numbers and said we would keep in touch. My family and I then headed back out of town heading east on that road and didn't pass another car for about five or more miles!

When you follow the hunches and urges given to you by your Guides, many opportunities are opened to you that you might have otherwise missed. Learn to listen and be aware of why things are happening around you that are synergistic. Remember, nothing is random and there is much information made available to us if we will only be attentive and respond to it.

Chapter 8 Dreams, Visits and Interpretations

One of the first ways a person usually receives contact from a loved one in spirit is in a dream. While sleeping, our consciousness is not in control; therefore, our subconscious is open to receiving these "visits." While we are awake, our brain is continually being bombarded with images, smells, sounds, tastes, new ideas, emotions, and so on. All that takes place in our life must be analyzed and filed appropriately. But when the brain is fully occupied protecting and monitoring the body and its functions, it cannot immediately file everything that is taking place. So it then stores certain items until the body is at rest or sleeps, when further attention can be given to sorting out this other information. If this sorting of information is interrupted due to the inability to sleep, the brain becomes stressed. Some dreams are the events of the day running through our brain sorting out different purposes. Sometimes the events overlay each other and the dream is a confused mixture of many images.

We all dream, yet not all dreams are remembered. We can periodically recall fragments, and sometimes the complete dream is remembered in detail. You can interpret dreams that stand out for their color, intensity, and impact. These include spiritual messages, past life recall, soul travel, and receiving visits from those on the other side. You can also translate and analyze your dreams to find hidden fears and other issues. A dream can vary from a factual report to a symbolic picture or combine fact and symbol. Below are some quick explanations of various dream states.

Recurring Dreams

Dreams that repeat can be preparation for a future event. When the dream is interpreted correctly so that its message is understood, it will likely stop. Recurring dreams can also be a sign of worry and confusion and are typically connected to emotional stress as an "indicator" that it is time to slow down and re-examine what is happening in your current life situation. Interpreting the dream will help you face the issue at hand and understand it.

Out-Of-Body Dreams

All people have a spirit which can leave its body while it sleeps. Some do this on rare occasions, while others do it very frequently. A dream of flying, being in another country or talking to another person who you know is far away are all likely to be out-of-body memories. A sudden waking with a heart jump or a dream of falling or spiraling down is usually a sign that a spirit has been out of its body while it sleeps.

Past Life Dreams

A person may remember a dream where they were living in a peculiar former time, usually wearing clothes from another century or even speaking a language they no longer understand. This is usually a sign that they have linked into one of their own past lives to regain knowledge by visiting specific events which will assist them in their present existence. On some occasions, upon waking, they recall that they were in the past but as an observer of what was occurring. These observing dreams are to remind and recall a past life, but without the need to re-experience it. You should examine the dream so you can understand the link related to present issues.

Information Dreams

Some people go to sleep with questions, problems, or in a mental struggle to resolve a difficult situation. These dreams usually appear in a symbolic form which, when interpreted, will help them find the answers they need. It is possible to concentrate on a specific question in the mind just before going to sleep, and then dream the answer.

Visitor/Visiting Dreams

Spirits on the other side can visit a sleeping person and communicate with your spirit consciousness. The person visited will recall a feeling of someone having been in the room, and partially remember conversations. It is possible, if we are worried about a person on earth, to ask our spirit to visit them while sleeping. Many of these dreams occur just before waking, usually between three and five in the morning. In fact, some people are quite convinced they were awake during the whole experience. When your spirit returns to its body, you usually wake up feeling dehydrated. Out-of-body activity uses energy and the body fluids. It is advisable to place a drink or bottle of water near your bed each night.

Those of you who find it hard to recall your dreams upon waking can train yourselves to do so. Put a pad and pencil near your bed so that you can reach it easily. When you wake in the morning with the memories of your dream still present, avoid any further thinking and just reach out and write down everything you can. If you allow your thought processes to begin, you will activate your brain and immediately start forgetting what you dreamt. When you have written what you can, sip your drink and return to sleep. Even if you have had another dream, you will still remember something. If you get into the habit of writing down your dreams this way, you will gradually retain more information on your own in the morning. What follows are some examples of various dreams friends and clients have sent me explaining "visits" they received from loved ones crossed over.

> **From Libby** (receiving a "visit" from her cousin Karri)
>
> "My dream started out at a beach, a sort of resort. Nothing fancy, there was a beach house and me and some of my friends were there. I mainly remember that my friend Michelle was with me. We walked through the beach area, looking at the waves and sand dunes, and there were sea oats growing on the dunes and waving in the breeze. It was a very casual, nice but low-key beach place, and it reminded me a lot of the outer banks of North Carolina.
>
> The next thing that happened was that I woke up and was in a double bed. (I'm still dreaming, but I'm waking up from a sleep IN MY DREAM.) It was early morning and the sun was coming through the windows. There were long, white curtains that were sort of gauzy and really billowy because the fabric was lightweight, like cotton, but they weren't blowing all over the place, more like rustling in the soft morning breeze. The walls of the room were whitewashed

wooden boards, not painted perfectly, like that "shabby chic" style that's been big for a few years. It was a cute, comfortable but not fancy room.

I lay in the bed for a little while and was thinking about getting up and going to the bathroom. Michelle was in the same bed with me and she was snoring a little bit. I figure that we were bunkmates and that the other gals we were vacationing with must have been in their rooms. I was lying there and my bladder was full, so I decided to quietly get up and go to the bathroom.

I cracked the door to the bedroom open and went to the bathroom. It was across the hall and down a few feet so the door wasn't directly across from the bedroom. The bathroom was a pretty good sized room. It had a sink to the right of the door – one of those white pedestal old-fashioned sinks that has the HOT and COLD porcelain knobs. There was a window directly across from the bathroom door that looked out across a porch and then onto the dunes and then the water. More white curtains hung on the window and it was cracked open at the bottom about 6 inches or so. The curtains were gently being pushed around by the slight breeze. To the left of the window was a wooden dressing table…more shabby chic. It was sanded white wood with a white cotton runner across the top, and it had a mirror attached to it. There was a sort of bench in front of it, and I don't really remember if it was wooden or upholstered but it was just a one-seater. On the other side of the dressing table and opposite the pedestal sink was a bathtub and shower. Nothing fancy, just like what you see in a hotel room, only there was no tile, the walls were wooden all around. It wasn't a giant bathroom, but it was a bit like a sitting room, because of the dressing table and there was room for several people to be in it without being really crowded.

I began brushing my teeth and for some reason, I opened the bathroom door. I walked over to it, still brushing, and opened the door out into the little hallway. As I turned and walked back toward the pedestal sink, the breeze caught the door and it very slowly started to close. I was afraid it was going to gather momentum and slam, so I took a big step toward the door and caught it with one hand, since I still was using the other one to hold my toothbrush in my mouth.

The door pulled very hard against me. Really hard, and I had to stop brushing and hold it with both hands. It continued to pull against me, not straining super hard but I remember thinking, "It's only a breeze, what's the deal? This is really hard to hold." And the door kept pulling, like it was pulling itself closed. For a second I thought I'd be stuck in the bathroom and have to climb out the window. It wasn't scaring me but it definitely was not a normal experience and I was a little weirded out by the whole thing.

After a few seconds of holding the door, it just stopped pulling and seemed to relax. I turned around and rinsed my mouth, put the toothbrush away and decided to get back in bed. I was a little unnerved but figured I was still sleepy and just not quite awake yet and that maybe it hadn't really happened.

I walked out of the bathroom, then looked back over my shoulder right before I walked back in to the bedroom. The bathroom door was moving back and forth slowly. It would go forward about 6 or 7 inches and then move back. From the angle I was at, I couldn't see the bathroom window to see how hard the curtains were blowing, but what I could see as the door moved back a second time was a person sitting at the dressing table.

All of my breath sucked in, and I stepped back against the wall. My heart was racing and I was very scared. The person's back was to me and the door was still moving slowly so I had only seen a little bit but it looked like the person had long brown hair. I was so scared that I became paralyzed.

From where I was pushed up against the wall, I could see into our bedroom and I could see Michelle's foot at the bottom of the bed. I started trying to get her attention, to call to her, to wake her up. My words were caught in my throat and I couldn't get anything out. I managed a very hoarse whisper and once I got her name out the first time, I just kept saying it over and over but my voice never got any louder. "Michelle, Michelle, Michelle."

I don't think I was whispering because I was afraid of the person in the bathroom. I didn't want them to know I was there. I had seen a person, a girl, I thought, and for some reason I didn't think it was a bad person. Maybe someone who was confused and in the wrong place but not a bad person. I wanted Michelle to wake up so we could confront the person together.

I heard Michelle rustling in the bed and saw her foot move as she rolled over toward the door. She said, "Lib?" and all I could do was keep saying her name in the whisper, "Michelle, Michelle." She sat up in bed, leaned forward and then was able to see where I was. My face must have been white because she suddenly looked very awake (not usual for her) and very scared, "What is it?" she whispered. I motioned for her to come toward me, and she slowly got out of bed, never taking her eyes off me. I put my finger to my lips and pointed down the hall toward the bathroom. We grabbed each other's hand and took a few steps toward the bathroom door that had stopped swinging and was now just slightly ajar.

We were side by side in front of the door, holding hands, and I reached out and pushed the door open to the right. There at the dressing table was a girl, with her back to us and she was in a white terry cloth bathrobe. Her back was to us and her long brown hair seemed sort of damp, like she had been in the shower with it up on her head and it got a little wet or she had been for a run and it was sweaty. Michelle and I stood there, holding hands, and then the girl turned around and smiled at us.

It was Karri.

My heart jumped into my throat and I took two steps toward her, and she stood up and we hugged. I held her so tightly. I could feel her ribs, and I could feel her wet hair and I just held her and held her. We were both laughing a little, and I heard Michelle saying over and over, "No way, no way." Karri pulled away from me a bit and turned toward Michelle and reached out to her and they both hugged. Then all three of us stood there holding on to each other, laughing, and I was crying a little bit but we were all smiling and it was so joyous and happy!

Karri sat down on the bench, and I remember me and Michelle sitting down on chairs or something. I don't know if they were in the bathroom and we just pulled them up or if one of us was on a chair and the other on a wooden step stool or what, but we were all at about the same level, looking at one another, bunched together and holding hands and more laughing.

Karri looked just like herself, except she had her hair pulled a little bit to the side and up by her forehead. It was secured with a hairpin that had a little enamel butterfly on it. It was a small barrette like something a little girl would wear, but I looked at it and it made so much sense to me because I knew Kayce's (Karri's sister) connection to butterflies. Karri had the robe wrapped loosely around her, and she was dewy and flushed.

I asked her how she was, and she said "fine" and that she was doing all right. She said there was some adjusting that she was doing and that it took some figuring out but that she thought she was getting it down. We laughed together, and it reminded me of her working hard in school to try and get good grades. I know it didn't always come easy to her and I thought, "Well, that's just like Karri. She's figuring out Heaven." And I was glad that there was that sameness, that consistency, and that she was her usual "figuring it out" self.

I told her how much I missed her, how much we all missed her. We felt so comfortable and at ease. There was no weirdness, only pure happiness.

I asked Karri what it was like and she paused. She seemed a bit uncertain about what to say, figuring it out, I guess. Then, after a few seconds, she said that she gets a little lonely sometimes. And my heart hurt for her. But she said it wasn't bad at all, not to hurt for her. "It's a very nice place, and there are wonderful people there." Again, she paused, "You know that I get shy sometimes. And that's what happens there. We're all together, and I get quiet and shy. And I think of everyone here." And then she said so earnestly, so forcefully, "When I come to see you, you <u>have</u> to let me in." I wasn't sure at first what she meant. And I must have looked confused because she said, "Like this, right now. This time you let the door open and you weren't afraid. That isn't the way it always is. Sometimes I come and the person I'm visiting doesn't know that I'm visiting or they don't know how to let me in. Please tell everyone that I am here and they should keep open to me. I want to see everyone so much."

I told her I would tell everyone and that I understood what she wanted me to do. And we hugged some more. I didn't cry, but I did hold her very, very hard. She laughed and said that I was squeezing her but it was okay. She said that she'd be back, and that she was happy to see

Michelle too and she thanked us again and again for "letting her in."

After all the detail of everything leading up to seeing her, the breezes, the furniture, the color of the walls -- there's no detail in my head of her leaving or of me and Michelle leaving.

I woke up and I just remembered that "I have to let Karri in" and "I have to keep open to her." When I lay in bed after waking up, at first, I sort of wished there had been a proper ending to the dream because I didn't want it to end abruptly. But then it occurred to me that Karri wanted to use the dream as an opportunity to tell me something that was important to her and that can help all of us see her. So the ending of the dream or the lack of an ending wasn't what was important. She didn't let me have an ending. She didn't want that. She wanted me to wake up with the most important part of her message the freshest thing in my head. I think, like she said, that she's figuring it all out and that she's getting better at it, so maybe that's why this time I was able to be open to her and I remembered everything so clearly. Maybe I'm getting better at it, too, and am more open to her. I don't know how or why that might be, but she told me to be open to her and to tell everyone else. So just know that she's here, she told me so, and she is figuring it out and maybe the rustling curtains are a sign that she's here. The breeze and the curtains and the door moving might have been a hint, I don't know. I do know that I'm going to be sleeping with the window cracked a lot more these days!

The following dreams can be very telling regarding "visits" as well as alluding to our higher purpose.

From Mary

I have a very interesting story to tell you about my daughter that I don't know what to think about it. Yesterday morning she was in the den waiting for me while I was making her lunch. So we are about to leave for school and as we get in the car she said, "Mamma there was a man in the room with me just now." I answered... "A man?" And she said, "Well he was in the window." I said, "There was a man looking in our window?" She said, "No it was a face by the window inside the house, and he had a beard and a mustache." Well, I pick up children for school and we were at our neighbor's house by this time so I stopped asking questions. So later that night on the way home I brought it up. She said it was a face and that it would come and go. It would get really clear and then blurred. She said he had a beard, mustache and long hair and then she proceeded to tell me he was smiling at her. Then she said, "Mamma...it looked like Jesus." She said, "He was really big too and kind of had a glow." I said, "You saw his body?" and she said "No, I just know he's big." So I asked her, "If you didn't see the body how did you see the glow?" And she said, "The glow was around the face." So at this point I play it cool and I said, "You know Taylor that we all have guardian angels and that you can talk to them anytime you want and they will answer you and always protect you and when you need help they are there for you." She goes on to say, "You mean like the way they help me in school?" So I said, "Yes, but what do you mean?" She said, "Well mamma, when I was doing my work I didn't know the answer so I asked for help and the answer came to my mind." She continued with, "I got all the answers right. Was that my angel helping me?" I asked her if she heard a voice and she said yes.

She also had a dream that she was walking through these beautiful woods and then all of a sudden there was this big mountain with crystals, a beautiful waterfall and a white horse standing by it. In this dream she said her friend from school told her you can play the games and if you win you can go to the next level and see beautiful things, but if you don't, you will have to go back and try again, then she woke up! I made her write it down. I want to start recording her dreams. She woke up one morning and while still half asleep she was saying, "Look mamma they are flying." She put her hand up in front of her and motioned like waves. Then she fell right back to sleep. I asked her later when she completely woke up what she thought about the people flying and she said she didn't remember.

I think she really sees things, since she's been 18 months old things have been happening to her. Not bad things, just things that are I believe, out of the ordinary.

Have a great day!
Love, Mary

From Denise

Hi Kathleen!

Hope this day finds you doing well, routine things around here as usual. But I do have a couple of questions on my mind that are bothering me after talking with my sister. She had a dream about our Dad. He was much slimmer like he was before he got sick, and was in a suit. Now my Dad was not a suit and tie man, so that was too weird. He told her to tell Mom he was all right and doing really good, but he was dressed up and said he was getting ready for another assignment. After letting this settle, I instinctively told her she had to tell Mom about her dream, that he came to her with a message and it wasn't just a dream. I told her I didn't think she really understood the magnitude of what her dream meant or was and that it was a very significant one. She didn't know why she had a dream like that. I said because she has opened herself up more to allow this to come in. And he knew a dream state is a safe place for her to accept and to bring messages. I went on to tell her he is getting ready to start a new life's journey and has graduated with high honors so to speak. (I hope I didn't assume about this).

My question is...at the time a reading is conducted, and a person has already gone on with another life, how will it affect the reading? How will it be different? Sorry Kat, I'm trying to explain this and I'm getting frustrated here. I feel like I should have this reading soon now, after what my sister told me about her dream, like I'm going to miss his presence being stronger or something if he isn't going to be there and starting a new journey. Are spirits fully intact when he/she goes in separate directions/assignments? Which leads me to think, spirit guides when they are guides, does that mean they do not start a new life elsewhere? But stay to help guide you? I haven't had a dream from him with any direct conversations or looking healthy, is it possible that I have shut myself off to it, without realizing? I've been waiting and wanting to see him in this light to feel more positive about his passing and to move on in someway. I don't know what to do with all this at times, and from what I have read or experienced it isn't any easier like I sort of thought. I feel this is teaching me a valued lesson in preconceiving this notion of it being easier somehow, and I was wrong about that.

Thanks Kathleen!
Denise

My answering correspondence:

Dear Denise:

Okay first off, you are right on about your interpretation about your sis's dream. Dad is on a new journey...one there in heaven and the spiritual plane. He may or may not be getting ready to incarnate again, but even if he was to incarnate and return again, no that doesn't mean he can't continue to speak to us in readings or that he isn't around you, he is. You agree that things are VERY complicated over there right? And that we know very little of how this all operates and how the spiritual and physical worlds work together. That said...I can tell you that in my readings, many come through and (also people who have had near death experiences) say that spirits have the ability to be in two places at once. That timelines don't really exist over there in the way that we know them here.

I also don't feel that you have in any way shut yourself off from Dad. It's just that you already are convinced of his existence in spirit so he doesn't have to prove it to you any more. You also have "graduated" to an awareness level of where you can just speak to him and know he'll answer. Then it's about trusting that really is his answer. You understand?

I do believe (based on my NDE studies) that even if our loved ones are spirit guides for us, they will continue to do this "job" until it is time for them to incarnate again. My sense of the dream is that your Dad is simply assisting and aiding many others *along* *with* his family members that are still here. Probably folks here on earth who are experiencing cancer as he did! Helping to put the right doctors, nurses, people, and places in their lives to ease pain, bring comfort to family members, and get the right treatments for these individuals. I hope this helps, and know I'm sending good thoughts your way!

Kat

This next dream exposes yet another phenomenon which those in spirit use to communicate with us. Light is a common tool utilized by those on the other side to make their existence known.

From Pam

Kathleen,

Hello from Houston, TX! You did a reading for me several months ago. It was a terrific experience, and the family members who I've shared my experience with have been blown away – after their eyebrows come down from the top of their heads! I have a quick question I'm hoping you can answer. A person who came through the strongest in our reading was my paternal grandfather who I was close with and my daughter is named after. I know from my conversation with you (and your book) that dreams are often a vehicle for contact with those who are no longer here with us. Since our reading, my grandfather has been present in a few of my dreams (no surprise) and I sense I'm supposed to do something with one piece of information I can't figure out.

In this dream, there was a flashing light (quickly, two times – like a diamond that catches light) that appeared several times. All I can remember is that I acknowledged to my grandfather (who was not there physically, but in the dream I knew he was in the room) that when the lights flashed, I knew it was him. Imagine a "Yes, I KNOW you're there!"

Do flashing lights have any sort of symbolic meaning in this context? I am not skilled at understanding this sort of communication and was hoping you could shed some light on this. (No pun intended!) Thanks in advance for the insight! And hope you're having a great summer!

Cheers,
Pam

Dear Pam:

Actually light is VERY significant and used
most often to communicate their existence to
us. Those who are gifted and/or develop their
ability of clairvoyance see this light when
awake also. Caught on film in a freeze frame
they appear as circles of light illuminating on
the outside with a visible nucleus of light in
the center. A clear bubble of light that glows.
It's called an orb. To the trained clairvoyant,
these orbs appear as small sparks of light. That
is spirit showing themself to you. Many
people see them unknowingly and assume it's
just their eyes playing tricks on them.

My guess is that your grandfather is preparing
you for what you will "see" when you are
awake, and that is the purpose of the dreams.

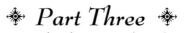

✤ *Part Three* ✤

How newfound awareness shapes lives.

Chapter 9 Developing Psychic
Reception Areas

Learning to tap into our own spiritual gifts is simple.
Making multi-dimensional communication possible between us
and the spirit world takes practice and patience, but it is available
to all of us who want to explore it. One of the first things you
need to identify is your psychic receptors, those tools that will be
your devices for language with those in spirit. Here are the main
four:

Psychic Feeling

Psychic feeling is most closely intertwined with our
physical sense of who we are. Its psychic reception area is at the
front your body, extending from the top of the diaphragm to just
below your navel. This area is where your solar plexus resides
and is the site of many nerve centers. The extrasensory
impressions you get here are those "gut" feelings you have.
These feelings are normally accompanied by uneasy physical
sensations such as butterflies, nausea or vague discomfort. The
more you listen to those "gut" sensations and go with your
"instinct" (what your Guides tell you), the more you will find
that you are protected, guided, and tuned in to your inner
feelings. This not only builds confidence in ourselves, but also in
our ability to understand how our Guides are leading and

directing us.

Psychic Intuition

Psychic intuition or knowing is another strong and definitive sense that we all too often take for granted. It is an inner awareness that is really unsupported by any particular inner sensation or external stimulus. In other words; "You just know!" The psychic reception area for intuition is the crown and top of your head. Picture a funnel with the small end on top of your head and extending upward, widening as it emerges. That funnel or psychic reception area is a direct conducting pathway to the corpus callosum (the nerve bundle which links the two hemispheres of your brain). To tap into your psychic intuition you need only think upward and note your impressions and intuitions. Most of us have had the experience of "knowing" what someone is going to say before he or she says it. Learn to practice this again and again and you will be surprised at how often you are correct in your impression or intuitive thought.

Psychic Hearing

The reception area for psychic hearing is, of course, on each side of your head, just above your ears. This is the area of the brain's temporal lobes (that section of the central nervous system that links to auditory processing). Psychic hearing is noticeable as inner sound such as words, phrases even sentences of inner dialogue which may come to you as if through psychic headphones. Sometimes, as we discussed before, the clairaudient impression of a familiar song may be meaningful. Your loved one is passing you a message through a means of communication they know you will recognize.

Psychic Vision

Last but not least, the psychic reception area for psychic vision will surprise you most. Do an exercise with me and close your eyes. Picture your vehicle and what it looks like. Now think of your workspace and what it looks like. You are experiencing clairvoyance or psychic vision. The images you just saw in your head are what images also look like when Spirit sends them to you. We think of them as "random" thoughts or messages, when in fact they are not random at all. Energy does not dissipate … it only changes form. Science tells us that there really is nothing that can be construed as random. Rather, every action in the universe causes an equal and opposite reaction. All matter and energy comes from a source of some kind!

You will notice that with your eyes closed, your visual awareness automatically shifts upward! It moves from eye level to the level of your forehead or where your crown chakra is located. This is why this chakra is often time referred to as the third eye. Open and close your eyes several times to experience this sensation paying close attention to the *shift* of where you sense your vision. This reception area is where you register clairvoyant impressions, like watching an internal television screen. When using clairvoyance, make sure you don't "force" the impression. If you try to force it, an image won't come. During meditation, simply "focus" instead on this psychic reception area. Mentally relax and ask for the pictures to be shown to you. Similar to peripheral vision, your psychic vision is just there, not forced, but yet exists for you to use when speaking to spirit.

What's next is learning how to meditate properly. Meditation is simply a ritual in a controlled fashion that will produce altered states of consciousness. A ritual is something we do in a set way time after time. Not every aspect of a ritual needs to be identical, but unless there are at least some actions, words, tools or meanings which are consistent from one action to the next, then the ritual will not have the impact that it is meant to have. Going to work or school every day is a ritual. Raising children or working on a hobby involves ritual.

Successful meditation is intentional bodily engagement in the paradigmatic forms and relationships of reality. Meditation brings not only the body, but also the mind to encounter the pure heightened awareness with the transcendental realm. Shifts in paradigm during meditation will have a cause and effect on your ability to achieve great strides in connecting with the ethereal plane. Be consistent in your rituals before, during and after meditation and you'll be successful in your ability to achieve great results.

While your whole day may consist of rituals, do a formal ritual (meditation) to deliberately set aside a time and space where you can focus on issues which are important to you without distractions from the outside world. Here a few ground rules that will help ensure your success.

> *** Create a separate area that is specifically chosen for meditation. This will create an energy power center that will increase in intensity over time.**

> *** Use candles, herbs, or incense to induce a comfortable relaxing environment.**

* Experiment with various meditations before settling on the one of your choice, such as an elevator rising through clouds, a palatial garden, or maybe a seashore. Then stay consistent with what you have constructed as your meditation ritual.

* Before any meditation do a protection exercise.

Some key points in successful meditation are: aligning your chakras and balancing your energies to work as one; raising your vibrations to a level high enough to meet spirit; being open to whatever you're shown by your guides or loved ones; and grounding yourself during and after each meditation. The body's vibrational frequency can be altered by internal and external influences. The following guided meditation is one method of protecting yourself from negative external vibrations. With practice you can learn to do this very quickly by using visualization and chanting the sound Aum (OM) in your mind.

Allow your body to become relaxed. Have the spine straight and the head upright. Close your eyes and take a slow breath in and out. Be aware of the flow of air through the nostrils. Let your hands and feet relax and the shoulders loosen.

Visualize your body surrounded by a large bubble. This membrane is strong and protecting. This is your aura. While you are inside, you can move around and the shape can change to accommodate this.

Although this is an invisible screen all around you, it is also a strong barrier from any negative vibration outside which would harm you.

You feel yourself protected inside your aura where nothing can harm you. In your mind you hear the sound Aum repeating and you know that this is raising your vibrational frequencies to a higher level, giving double protection to your aura. Picture yourself inside your aura safe and sheltered from harm.

This protection exercise is very important when doing any form of meditation. You are opening your channels up and inviting spirit from another dimension in so you only want to attract that which is of the highest good. After protecting yourself, then begin the formal process of building a personal meditation. I've created a shortened version of one for you here:

Begin by offering a prayer, in which you ask your Maker to be with you, leading you to that information that is of the highest good, surrounding you in this place with the impenetrable white light, and raising your vibrations and your awareness to the highest possible level in each and every moment.

Close your eyes and take deep breaths, slowly inhaling through the nose and exhaling through the mouth. This is the practice of pranayama (or breathwork). This rhythmic breathing technique will relax the muscles and stimulate your brain with increased oxygen levels. Begin to visualize energy running up and down the outline of your body in a white and golden color. Beginning at your left outside foot, and running up the outside of the left of the body, and across the top of the head, and back down the right side - sort of making an outline or silhouette of your body in this energy.

Visualize this liquid light and see it beginning to spread out and encompass you in the form of an egg so that you are in this embryo of energy. This egg is your aura.

Once you feel that you are completely encased in this egg or cocoon of light, inhale deeply, taking in some of this light and sending it down through your entire body. Visualize this golden white light filling you with positive, warm, spiritual energy. Now exhale dark gray, black, negative energy. All the stresses of the day, all the negative encounters you had which may still be stuck in your aura are leaving you. Visualize this negative energy as it leaves your body and your aura, never to return again. Continue deeply filling your lungs and body with this liquid light, and exhaling negative energy.

Next, visualize every cell in your body as a *vibrational* structure and inhale golden light that disperses through every single cell of your body. Your hair, your nails, your skin, every cell in your body is now going to be *activated* with this golden white light.

Take this energy down through the seven chakras and the soles of your feet and anchor them to the center of the Earth. You can visualize the center of the Earth as a golden star, a ball of light, a molten mass. Now anchor this energy through the seven chakras and your feet, down to the center of the Earth, and back up to your feet again. Breathe out down into the Earth, inhale back up from the Earth. Now you have anchored this energy within you, and grounded it to this earthly plane.

Know that in this moment this energy raises its vibrations. Visualize as this golden white light falls around you it begins to spin around your feet and ankles. Feel the vibrational energy as it spins faster and faster climbing up your legs. Continue seeing your vibrational energy twirling around you encompassing your entire body. This golden white light raising your vibrations begins spinning faster and faster to meet spirit.

Looking through your mind's eye, see this golden white light grow brighter and brighter. So bright that you normally wouldn't be able to look at it, but no matter how bright it gets, it is not painful to your eyes. You are protected from any harm and this spiritual light is warm, inviting and soothing. Now see your loved ones and Spirit Guides coming into view to meet you in this bright light. Visualize them as they approach from the distance getting closer and clearer. Ask them questions and wait for their response. Know that you are connecting with them and that they truly see and hear you. They know your thoughts and desire to speak with you. Feel the warmth of their love surround you. Take a few moments to speak with them.

After you are finished, thank your loved ones and Spirit Guides for coming to visit you and now slowly start bringing your energy back down. Visualize the golden white light encircling you, slowing and winding down. Feel this spiritual energy slowing the vibrations and spiraling downward as it falls to your feet.

End by offering a prayer in which you thank your Maker, your Spirit Guides, and especially your loved ones who came to be with you during meditation.

Keep a record in either a journal or diary of any and all information you experience during meditation. This will be a vital part of your ability to learn and recognize specific signs and symbols your Guides and loved ones use to communicate with you. You can't possibly remember everything that takes place in all your meditations week after week, month after month. You will however have the advantage of flipping back through your journal as you begin to see synchronous events and information begin to unfold in order to determine how your Guides and loved ones speak to you.

Chapter 10

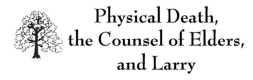

Physical Death, the Counsel of Elders, and Larry

Much is spoken about dying, death and the process we must each go through. Death, like everything else, has its categories. Upon death, most people go through a myriad of spiritual events before entering into the heavenly realms. In explaining the various transition processes experienced, remember that these are generalizations based on findings while studying NDE's.

People who are of a wicked nature or have led a life of immorality, instead of experiencing the tunnel and bright light upon death, are sent through what's referred to as the "side door". They enter into an abyss of empty, joyless, nothingness for a brief period of time. They have to reflect upon their actions, and are usually instructed that they will be reincarnated again to attempt to live life in a better manner.

People who commit suicide are sent to a "holding place" sort of like a purgatory. They must revisit key events in their life again and again, shuffling around slowly, determining their outcome. With the help of other wiser spirits who are there to guide them, they grow from this experience to an understanding and acceptance that they cheated by terminating their contract early. Once that understanding takes place, they then make the choice to embrace their Maker and move on to the light. We each have a chart, contract, or life record of what we are to accomplish with each incarnation. This chart or contract contains life lessons and choices such as what role we will play in our existing family. Karma and other ties to our previous incarnations help to determine exactly which lessons we will try to conquer and learn. Keep in mind that ideologically on the other side everything is wonderful, cosmic in understanding, unlimited, and comprised of total peace. So when we sat down with the counsel of elders and our Master Guide to lay out our current contract we were much braver and had a sense of invincibility. It's no wonder we say to ourselves, "I can't believe I chose this before coming here."

The majority of us have plodded our way through life, and when it is our time to transition to the other side, we go through a tunnel and towards the light of our Maker. We return home to the place we came from on the other side. Here, we have a reunion with family and friends who have departed before us. After the reunion, most of us are led by our Master Guide to a structure called the **"Hall of Wisdom."** In this sacred room, we see our lives flash before us in what appears to be a three-dimensional holographic screen. Once we have fully evaluated our lives, we are debriefed in an orientation process. In other words, we are asked to judge ourselves. This is when we discuss the lifetime just previously lived. We then meet with our Guides who discuss with us ways of atoning for previous mistakes and amending our behavior to grow properly. One way of atonement might be to have an activity assigned to us while in spirit to assist someone handicapped who is still here on earth if we were once discourteous to someone with disabilities while we were in the earthly plane. We also receive help in the Hall of Wisdom if we were unprepared for our crossing over into the spirit realm because of a sudden or shocking death.

Once a person has adjusted to the transition, they can then visit a place called the **"Hall of Records"** where historical data is stored such as the records of everyone's past lives or our own contract or record. Another beautiful structure is the **"Hall of Justice"** where people go before a "Council of Elders" who are highly advanced spokespersons of our Maker. They help us decide how we are to progress further into the spirit realm.

Reincarnation takes place when a spirit recognizes the need for further advancement and therefore chooses to return to earth to gain this soulful knowledge. With the help of a Master Spirit Guide, they decide on an incarnation which will meet their goals. They then proceed to the Hall of Justice where they meet once again with the Council of Elders. Here, the Council prepares the spirit by assisting with choices of specific lessons, trials and experiences to encounter while in this embodiment. When they are ready to incarnate, their family and friends are gathered together to bid farewell. Once they have said their good-byes, people are then taken to a place where they are eased into a deep sleep. The journey into the womb begins and a new life is born on earth.

It's important for us to realize that although we consider physical death as a negative, it is actually the beginning of the transition to a re-birth into a spiritual existence. I have been to many funerals where it is a celebration of the deceased's life rather than a morbid goodbye to the newly departed. Of course not all deaths are expected or have they come as a result of positive circumstances. But for those whose passing was expected or those passing under natural circumstances, death can be used to gain much closure and provide comfort to those still here, knowing their loved one no longer has to be weighted down by a physical body and that they now have the freedom and ability to be with all.

I'd like to share a story with you of my Uncle Marvin who passed recently from Alzheimer's disease. Marvin was residing in a long-term health care facility because my Aunt

Janet could no longer care for him due to his advancing illness. It was seldom that Marvin would recognize Janet when she came to visit. Regardless, she would visit him daily. One evening around midnight, she was in the middle of taking a shower when her phone rang. She sensed immediately it was something to do with Marvin. Running to the phone she answered it, standing there naked, dripping wet. Sure enough, it was the nurse's station calling to inform her that Marvin had coded and to please come to the heath care facility as soon as possible. Janet threw on some clothes and drove there as fast as she could. When she arrived at Marvin's room she saw him lying on his bed, fast asleep. They were able to revive him and had placed a tube in his throat so he could breathe. The doctor began to speak to Janet as she stood there mesmerized.

"Janet, I have to tell you something. Marvin said the strangest thing as we revived him."

"What's that?" Asked Janet.

"He said to me... 'Hey doc, don't turn around...my wife is standing there naked at the end of the bed!' "

Janet about fell over. The doctor told her there was more. He let her know that Marvin, before coding, kept saying that someone named Maynard was calling him. He just kept say Maynard again and again. "Who is Maynard?" the doctor asked. Janet replied... "His deceased brother!"

They both were astonished. Janet stayed with Marvin for several hours then returned home for some sleep. The next day as Janet walked into Marvin's room for her daily visit, he quickly turned toward her and shouted "Janet! It's so good of you to come see me." She cried as she held him in amazement. That weekend Marvin passed onto the other side. Janet is, however, very comforted in the gifts she received from God and

Marvin those last few days. She took comfort that even in the advanced stages of a mind stealing disease Marvin's soul knew who it loved and who it had shared this life with, and it immediately went to that individual at the time of passing. She took comfort that his near death experience seemed to jolt his consciousness enough to recognize her in an awakened state. And, most importantly, she knows that he is with his brother Maynard, happy and content.

Bringing in Larry Hastings...

It's common for people who, like Larry Hastings, experience an NDE and come back to this plane with their psychic and spiritual gifts heightened. We all have spiritual gifts. We are all beings of energy that possess varying degrees of intelligence based on our growth as well as the rate in which we grow and learn. Sometimes our Guides are very definitive in giving us direction, which will help to increase this knowledge and further our spiritual advancement.

I met Bob and Patty Dean for the first time when they attended one of my gallery sessions. This is a meeting room with usually about 20 to 40 people in attendance. The focus of the gallery is to help those present to learn how to connect on their own to those on the other side. Then I do live readings for those in the audience. Although Bob and Patty did get a few messages that first time, they were rather quiet and I could sense they were what I affectionately call "newbies" to the process. As time marched on, they began attending more gallery sessions and we became good friends. I would later discover their quest to understand the mysteries of the spirit world and its parameters. As our relationship progressed, Bob began sharing with me pieces of a journal he had been writing to document his experiences. I found it fascinating that he would be so diligent in keeping such accurate documentation over such a long period of time. As far as I could tell he'd been working on it for at least 2 years!

Recognizing the tremendous thirst of others desiring to know and understand what he had experienced, Bob agreed to publish his journal in a book. What happened next was amazing. As we began collaborating on this manuscript, our Guides were immediately active and very direct in providing us with signs. Bob told me all about his friend Larry Hastings who had a very intense NDE. I suggested that we might consider having Larry contribute stories of his experience and subsequent events that took place after his NDE. Bob agreed, saying that he would share our idea for the book with Larry. Bob called me a few days later to say that Larry was open to discussion about contributing to the project. "Good, I thought…things seemed to be rounding out nicely."

I began to feel some anxiety, since I was accustomed to this 'feeling' when my Guides are trying to alert me about something. I consulted with the 'crew' and was told that this project was very important. When the anxiety wouldn't go away a few days later, I contacted Bob and asked him if he'd be open to fly to Lebanon, Missouri to meet with Larry. I figured if I met with this man, maybe my Guides would calm down a bit. Like a doting mother, they were hounding me to get moving on this. Bob said yes, and we agreed to look at airfares and get back with each other. That very next day, he received a phone call from Larry telling him that he would be flying to Dallas on the weekend to drop off some passengers, and he would have a few hours to meet with us. Bob started to chuckle and explained to Larry that the "folks" were already starting to wave their mystical influence over us. When Bob called me with the news I about fell over. "Okay" I said, "I guess we know who's in charge don't we?" We just laughed, then worked out a time to get together.

Now most psychic mediums will tell you that they are indeed the biggest skeptics. We are continually asking for proof and validations from those on the other side, even in circumstances where the signs are very clear and direct. But that also explains why we believe so strongly in the communication process that takes place between physical entities and those in spirit. We receive those validations over and over until we're satisfied. Our Spirit Guides understand our skepticism and allow for our lack of comprehension. They repeatedly work hard to offer us signs we'll recognize in order to keep us on our path and help us in learning what we came here to learn. Having said that, I requested a sign the next morning while in the shower preparing to go meet Larry and Bob. I assembled the 'crew', as I lovingly call my Guides, and asked them for a definitive sign that I was heading in the right direction. (FYI...when I do this they habitually send me a heart in some form to let me know I'm on track.) As the steam built up in the bathroom, I noticed only two marks on the glass door of the shower – two perfect hearts. In a gasp I said out loud, "You've got to be kidding!" I smiled and went on with my shower. Not accepting such a quick response from them, I asked for another sign. A few minutes later I was still getting nothing from them clairvoyantly or clairaudiently, but as I stepped out of the shower I again glanced at the door to see that the largest heart had now turned into a HUGE capital letter Y and the other smaller heart had disappeared. It's not that I didn't want to believe but again I just smirked and tossed it off to luck and creative steam.

I said out loud once again, "You'll have to do better than that. Be straightforward and precise...spell it out! I need to know if Larry is supposed to be part of this effort." Just then the phone rang. It was my older son. As I opened the nightstand in our bedroom to write down some information he was giving me, my eyes fell on a piece of paper. I was stunned. There lying on top was a sales receipt from a store called LARRY'S SHOES! Now in the fifteen years I've been with my husband, I've never known him to keep sales receipts in the nightstand. I quietly smiled to myself and uttered, "Well alright then...guess we know how the crew feels about this meeting." To me it was clear: they were telling me I would be walking in Larry's shoes in the book. After meeting Larry that day, he informed me that he would be happy to contribute to the book, yet he would rely on me to write everything down. You see Larry doesn't do email, or take a fancy to using a computer. He made it clear that he expected Bob and I to write his story...in other words, walk in his shoes!

The three of us met in the General Aviation lounge (for corporate and private jets only) at DFW Airport and Larry told us his story. He spoke with clarity and distinction and there was no doubt or hesitancy in his voice. This is how he described his NDE to me...

In 1980 Larry Hastings operated an air charter and air ambulance flight service in Lander, Wyoming. One flight involved a man that had fallen from an oil-drilling rig into the equipment below. He was badly bashed and broken. As Larry and an ambulance attendant were loading the 250-pound worker into the airplane, the ambulance attendant tripped and dropped his end of the stretcher. Having the head end of the stretcher, Larry couldn't let go without causing the man any more trauma, which could have been deadly. The force required to hold the stretcher caused pain in Larry's lower back.

As Larry, the patient, and two flight attendants arrived in Denver, they were met by an ambulance that was to take the injured workman to the Denver hospital for surgery. As he tried to exit the pilot's seat, Larry discovered that he could barely move due to extreme back pain. Larry was flown home on the same stretcher that was used by the injured worker.

Larry was admitted to the hospital and given a milogram, which would tell the orthopedic doctors exactly where the problem was located. This milogram was different though. It used a new water-soluble dye that would dissipate in the body, unlike the normally used oil-based dye that had to be removed. The advantage was that the water-soluble dye would make the procedure less invasive.

The procedure itself went well, but after 24 hours of high fluid intake with his head raised in the bed, Larry developed extreme headaches and hallucinations from the dye which had been used. Five other patients given the same type of milogram were experiencing the same conditions. Larry had to stop eating and taking fluids, and an IV was induced.

After the third day, Larry occasionally became conscious between the headaches and hallucinations and asked the male nurse on duty to do something.

"I can't take this anymore! Please give me something to help!" Larry pleaded.

The nurse informed him that he would call the doctor on duty to see what he could do. The nurse came back again with a syringe. He told Larry that he was putting Demerol into his IV in an attempt to provide some relief. Almost immediately, Larry felt a warm sensation traveling up his arm to his chest. It was an amazing sensation. After days of suffering, he was finally without pain. The nurse said "I'll be back in a while to check on you."

A nurse named Susan returned a few minutes later and asked, "Larry...how are you doing?" Larry could hear her quite clearly, but he could not respond verbally or open his eyes. She shook his knee and grabbed his wrist to check for a pulse, then laid her head on his chest to listen for a heartbeat. She then said "Oh my God...he's dead!!" "I am not dead," Larry protested mentally. "I just can't talk or open my eyes."

Susan ran from the room and returned with some other staff members. As he lay there his body began to feel very light. He felt like he was floating and felt himself begin to rise closer to the ceiling. He was sure he was hallucinating. As he hovered over them there in the room, Larry then felt himself float out of the hospital room. He immediately began to experience a falling sensation at a very high rate of speed through a dark tunnel toward a light that was getting increasingly brighter. So bright that it was as if he were staring straight at the sun yet he felt no pain in his eyes. The bright white and golden light now engulfed him and he found himself standing before a presence of a supreme being. A tremendous sense of peace and pure bliss overwhelmed him. Larry had an instantaneous sense of awareness about the entire universe, how it worked, why it worked, a clear understanding of the laws of physics, and a sense that all knowledge was available to him.

The presence was communicating with him, yet he did not actually hear anything. It was more like telepathy. Larry strained to look at the being, but he could only make out a silhouette. He was told that his time on earth was not yet finished, and that he would be returning there to finish his lessons. Larry tried to disagree and begged to stay, stating that he liked it there at "home" and in no way wanted to go back to such a difficult existence. As he expressed these thoughts to the being, he was again told it was necessary to return until his tasks were completed. However, the being then assured him that he would be guided through his remaining time.

Larry then awoke in the hospital bed totally awake and aware of his surroundings...*twenty minutes after he was pronounced dead.* The next day, the back surgery was completed and successful.

Larry said that, in looking back, he really needed that "wake-up call". He had been given the opportunity of a lifetime to touch and understand the "Other Side". He was no longer afraid of physical death, and he was looking forward to the day he could return home. Yet...few people seemed interested in hearing about his experience. Friends and family just wanted him to return to *normal*, yet he knew he was *not* normal. He had changed.

Shortly after Larry's NDE and recovery from back surgery, he returned to his flight operations business. One busy afternoon a man by the name of Edward Becvarik asked to see Larry. He was interested in getting flight instruction for an instrument rating and he wanted Larry to be his instructor. Larry informed Mr. Becvarik that he didn't have time for instructing but he could refer someone else. Mr. Becvarik insisted that he would only take lessons from Larry because his wife Carol, who was a prominent psychic, was told by her Spirit Guide to move from Glenwood Springs, Colorado to Lander, Wyoming to take flight instructions only from Larry Hastings. They had already moved and were ready for the lessons. Larry had developed quite a reputation for himself in this business and was known for his high sense of professionalism.

Larry gave in, and provided Ed the instrument training he needed. Their relationship as friends grew and over time Carol Becvarik taught Larry the benefits of about being a vegetarian. She demonstrated to him the proper foods to eat in a healthy diet of fruits, vegetables and other naturals sources of protein. She explained to Larry the many benefits of being on this type of eating regimen and the effects of it increasing his *alertness* and *gifts*. Even more importantly, she introduced Larry to automatic writing. Carol told Larry that automatic writing was the key to direct communications with your Spirit Guides. The Supreme Being he met during his NDE had assured him he would receive assistance when he returned to the earthly plane. Larry was very interested in learning a way to speak with them. After some practice, automatic writing indeed began working for Larry and through this he became introduced to his Spirit Guide "Joshua". Joshua has helped Larry to *see* many things, provided encouragement when necessary, and aided in defining for Larry what some of his life lessons and purpose is here on this plane of existence.

Larry's belief system is simple. The soul lives forever; religions do not exist on the Other Side; and we all answer to the same spiritual hierarchy. The universe is a circle. There is no time measurement there…just infinite existence.

He has also learned that we graduate to higher spiritual levels with each incarnation. Every soul has free will and can choose to advance or remain stuck on one level. The levels are based on what knowledge we have gained in any physical existence, and also upon the growth in unconditional love and the desire to help others.

Time has a different meaning to Larry than it does to ordinary people. To quote him, "I don't go by anyone else's clock. I do things in my own time frame when I think they should be done." That's not to say that Larry doesn't follow routines or that he doesn't adhere to certain schedules, because he does. What Larry means is that he no longer feels a prisoner to time. He is totally comfortable with what he has to accomplish because he *knows*. He knows that he is ready to go "home" whenever it's necessary. In the meantime, he will continue to work on achieving the best possible human state that he can and be devoted to his family. He says he feels less anger than he did before his NDE. He doesn't bottle up emotions anymore, but rather releases them and no longer feels trapped. He can work with his emotions much more sensibly now.

When asked about some of the more important lessons that he's learned while going through this experience, he says he was told by the Supreme Being that we all need to practice not responding to the negative influences placed in front of us. Instead, we need to take steps to change or sidestep what is causing the negative energy.

Larry told me that if you ask the right questions, your Spirit Guide would answer. Meditation is essential to higher spiritual awareness. He continued... "I am always traveling downstream. I can make choices but I am still heading in the same direction. You should always strive to improve yourself, be kind to others, and make a difference on this earthly plane. If you follow this belief system, all sorts of new opportunities will open up to you, and your life will be filled with joy."

In conclusion, here is a summary of what Larry learned from his Near Death Experience:

You come back here to advance.

You want to get it right so you don't have to come back.

You don't get judged ...*you* judge yourself on the other side.

You alone have to live with whatever your behavior was while on earth.

There is no escape; you live forever, so you better get it right.

Chapter 11 Answering Tough Questions

In my experience as a medium I am witness to countless examples of what life must be like on the other side and other anomalies in the universe by virtue of what comes through in the readings I do for others. After hundreds of sessions, I have drawn certain conclusions leading me to have specific beliefs on various subjects ranging from reincarnation to what folks in the spirit world do in their spare time. I've chosen the most commonly asked questions, and hopefully they are ones that you have also asked yourself. Please note that these are my opinions based on my experiences in connecting those here with those on the other side, as well as my private encounters in dealing with spiritual phenomena.

How do we blend organized religion with what people refer to as paranormal spirituality? Generally speaking, most of us practice some form of organized religion. Sometimes that religion is based on how we were raised. Other times, it is something we chose ourselves because of our own convictions or experiences. Whatever the reason, there is a great deal of comfort in the structure and clarity of the rules and regulations which outline that basic faith. We know what is expected of us and we can determine how we want to live based on those rules.

Society creates rules we must live by. Without rules and laws there would be complete anarchy. Rules are good. There is an old saying however…"Power corrupts and absolute power corrupts absolutely." Man from the beginning of time has tried to outdo each other. Men put in place the rules and laws of each individual faith. Through the inspiration of their Supreme Being, each faith was built on scriptures, doctrines, and other documentation of prophets who believed they spoke to God and thereby interpreted his laws. I am a practicing Catholic. I love my faith and its rituals such as the Rosary. I do believe that all religions have more similarities than differences and all point to a hierarchy that is in place to lead us *home*, a symbolic offering of the path to righteousness.

But cultural and social differences dictate what is available for our scope of consciousness to grasp. Therefore organized religion will contain variables. As children of God, we have do determine which of those variables are right for us. I choose to believe that our God is an all-loving entity. My intense study of near death survivors shows me that there is only one true faith and that is faith in Him and that we continually strive to elevate ourselves to the likeness of Him spiritually. That means using *all* the gifts God gave us, those both seen and unseen. Condition yourself to know that you have the right to believe in what is shown to you from those on the other side. It is God and they who are trying to prove to you that life exists beyond physical death.

How do we determine if it was really our loved one's "time" to cross over to the spirit realm at physical death? This is a hard one to explain because of its sensitive nature. So many theories and opinions vary on this topic. The question over the timing of a physical death arises when it is abrupt, accidental, sudden illness, or in cases of murder or suicide for example. In cases where the individual dies from natural causes or passes in their sleep, or from old age, the death is more readily accepted as, "It was their time to go." In readings, the spirit coming through will often time relay how, why and when they crossed over. There seems to be a consensus that even though the physical death may have occurred in a sudden and unexpected fashion, the physical passing was often determined by that individual while in spirit form before reincarnating. It was in their akashic record or contract as a self-fulfilling prophecy.

In all things, teaching exists. On rare occasions the spirit will be frank about the fact that they were unaware of what was to come and that they took no responsibility for their crossing. My suggestion on how to tell the difference, or in trying to determine if it was your loved one's 'time', is to examine what led up to the time of their passing. Glance back at the last few months, weeks or even days and hours just prior to their physical death and look for signs or clues they might have given. On a soul's level, most people will behave out of the ordinary just prior to a crossing, either by the things they say or by the things they do. They may indicate out of the blue that they want to write up a will, or they start giving possessions away for no apparent reason. I don't want to alarm anyone, but just use discretion when you see your friends or relatives exhibiting such behavior. Many people say after the fact that indeed those signs were there. That doesn't mean we should try to change destiny. Of course we want to protect our loved ones and keep them safe, but I do believe that if it's their time to go, it's their time to go.

How does a medium, or anyone for that matter, have the ability to speak to a spirit if that spirit has been reincarnated? The universe is to itself as it is to the universe. We are all individual parts of a larger whole. Energy begets energy and doesn't dissipate; it only changes form. Are you getting the idea? It is challenging for us to comprehend objects, articles and entities in terms of being multi-dimensional. Living in a linear existence, we are conditioned to see things in three-dimensional ways. Given that energy from a living source never goes away, like a beam of light in the galaxy, it will bend its shape, twist and even separate into smaller rungs but it won't just disappear. This living source of energy, then, has the ability to be in two places simultaneously. Time doesn't exist as we know it on the other side. What is before is also after. We must assume, then, that although an entity or spirit has incarnated to another physical existence, its energy still resides near those it loved and can, on a specific level, expound that love through communication from the spirit dimension.

Why do deceased loved ones whom we desperately want to contact not show us any signs that they are okay and around us if there is an afterlife? There may be many reasons in answering this question. One reason is that although the contact is desired, your consciousness deep down is afraid of the unknown. Confronted with a sudden vision of a loved one can and usually is very alarming at first. So we tend to unknowingly shut off our ability to be open to spirit contact. Another reason might be that we are very open to contact yet we are missing the signs they give us because of lack of knowledge of what to look for.

Research and discover the common ways people in spirit use to reach out to us. They may also simply be busy on the other side helping others or furthering their growth. I have had some relatives of mine wait until what seems like years after their passing to make contact with me, and then there are others who wasted no time after their passing to let me know that they are around. The variables are far and wide, and to this day I am not one hundred percent certain what it is that denotes the ability to contact someone in the earthly plane. I do know this: that when a loved one in spirit desires to make contact it is usually in a manner that you will comprehend and understand. It wouldn't serve their purpose to make it difficult for you to grasp. The purpose of contact is to validate for you that they still exist in spirit.

When two individuals are educated in spiritual communication in the same way, what determines one person's ability to be so much greater than the next? We all differ in how we perceive information...some learn visually, some learn audibly, etc. Mediumship and the ability to raise your level of consciousness is *available* to everyone. We can all paint, but we may not all be a Monet. Each one of us possesses *gifts* that are part of who we are. Whether you are more sensitive in seeing or hearing can differentiate you from someone else. Our spiritual or psychic senses are simply an extension of our physical senses. Clairaudience is the ability hear, clairvoyance is the ability to see, clairalience is the ability to smell, clairhambience is the ability to taste, and clairsentience is the ability to sense or feel information from spirit. By finding a good instructor or spending some time at your local library or bookstore you can teach yourself how to raise your level of awareness. Typically an individual is stronger in three out of the five senses but continuing practice in increasing your gifts will help to strengthen your overall ability.

I hope this book has shed light on the possibilities for true realization and provided you with a better understanding of the ability to achieve higher spiritual awareness. In putting this book together we all worked diligently to convey our developing philosophies as we continue to experience the magnificent and spectacular events that cross our paths. They say information is power...and I believe that to be true. I also believe that in your search for information about what else is out there, your ability to let go of standard limitations and your openness to unobstructed thinking will greatly increase your awareness of what the soul can do. What you perceive you can achieve!

To reach Bob Dean or Kathleen Tucci, or for more information on their seminars, lectures, or appearance schedule, you can write to them at:

　　Bob Dean / Kathleen Tucci
　　2828 Parker Road, Suite B106e
　　Plano, Texas 75075

Or visit their website at www.connectingtospirit.com

If you would like to submit an inspirational story or discuss any of the experiences in the book, please mail to the above address or email to:

bobdean@connectingtospirit.com

or

kathleen@kathleentucci.com

Resources

"During my spiritual journey I continuously searched for books and internet sites that would help me to advance and gain more knowledge of how the spirit dimension works. The following are some of the sources that I found to be most helpful. For anyone planning on pursuing their own spiritual journey, these sources would be a good start."

Bob Dean

Books

ONE LAST TIME ... John Edward

John Edward discusses how he first discovered then gradually developed his psychic ability to foretell events and communicate with the deceased. He also empowers people to tune into their own psychic abilities, and read and understand signs of spiritual contact they may be experiencing every day without even knowing it.

HELLO FROM HEAVEN ... Bill and Judy Guggenheim

Research book about after-death communication - actual ADC experiences, death and dying, life after death, and the afterlife.

MANY LIVES, MANY MASTERS ... Brian Weiss, MD

One of the best books on reincarnation, past life regression, and how that activity connects to the spirit world.

WE ARE ETERNAL ... **Robert Brown**

What the spirits on the other side tell him about life after death and spirit communication.

EMBRACED BY THE LIGHT ... **Betty J. Eadie**

One woman describes her profound near death experience.

THE AFTERLIFE EXPERIMENTS ... **Gary Schwartz, PhD.**

This riveting narrative, with its electrifying transcripts, puts the reader on the scene of a breakthrough scientific achievement: contact with the beyond under controlled laboratory conditions. Dr. Schwartz was forced by the overwhelmingly positive data to abandon his skepticism, reaching some startling conclusions.

SÉANCE or SECOND CHANCE ... **Suzane Northrop**

One of the mediums who took part in the Arizona Experiments. Why you were born, what death is, and why there can be so much pain in-between . . . if you question your choices, aren't sure about the people you attract into your life, and would love to stop making the same "mistakes" over and over again.

VIBRATING TO SPIRIT ... **Kathleen Tucci**

In her book *Vibrating To Spirit*, Kathleen illustrates for us what lies beyond our own visible world and presents inspiring stories with testimony of her amazing psychic ability to communicate with loved ones on the other side. Kathleen also shows you how you can make that connection with the spiritual realm on your own, giving you the tools necessary to empower you on your own spiritual journey and tune into your own psychic abilities.

Websites

http://www.connectingtospirit.com

http://johnedwardtalk.org

http://www.near-death.com

http://victorzammit.com

http://www.after-death.com

http://www.kathleentucci.com

Movies

What Dreams May Come

Starring Robin Williams, Cuba Gooding Jr., Annabella Sciorra, Max von Sydow, Rosalind Chao, Jessica Brooks Grant. One of the best commercial films to depict what the 'other side' is really like in terms of interpretation.

The Sixth Sense

Starring Bruce Willis. A boy who communicates with spirits that don't know they're dead seeks the help of a disheartened child psychologist.

Printed in the United States
89146LV00002B/562-576/A